I0022217

Comparative Legislative Studies Series

Malcolm E. Jewell
Editor

Legislative Party Campaign Committees in the American States

Anthony Gierzynski

THE UNIVERSITY PRESS OF KENTUCKY

Copyright © 1992 by the University Press of Kentucky

Scholarly publisher for the Commonwealth, serving Bel-
larmine College, Berea College, Centre College of Ken-
tucky, Eastern Kentucky University, The Filson Club,
Georgetown College, Kentucky Historical Society, Kentucky
State University, Morehead State University, Murray State
University, Northern Kentucky University, Transylvania
University, University of Kentucky, University of Louisville,
and Western Kentucky University.

Editorial and Sales Offices: Lexington, Kentucky 40508-4008

Library of Congress Cataloging-in-Publication Data
ISBN: 978-0-8131-5278-3
Gierzynski, Anthony, 1961–
    Legislative party campaign committees in the American states /
Anthony Gierzynski.
        p.   cm. — (Comparative legislative studies series)
    Includes bibliographical references and index.

    1. Campaign funds—United States—States.   2. Political parties-
-United States—States.   I. Title.   II. Series.
JK1991.G53   1992
324.7′8′0973—dc20   91-26935

This book is printed on acid-free paper meeting the requirements of the American National Standard for Permanence
of Paper for Printed Library Materials. ∞

For Kelsey

Contents

Figures and Tables

Foreword

This volume is the first in the Comparative Legislative Studies Series, which is designed to serve as a focal point for research on legislative studies in the United States and abroad, at national and subnational levels.

Controversy over how campaign funds are raised and spent, and over the sheer cost of elections, is permeating American politics. As state legislatures grow more professional, even legislative elections are becoming expensive in many states.

Anthony Gierzynski describes the development and behavior of campaign committees operated by legislative party leaders or caucuses to raise and allocate funds for legislative candidates. Using data from a number of representative states, he examines the criteria used for targeting districts and allocating funds. Unlike political action committees, which give disproportionately to entrenched incumbents, legislative party committees fund races that are expected to be close and support both incumbents and challengers on that basis. As a consequence, legislative elections have become more competitive, and these committees may actually strengthen legislative party leadership and cohesion.

MALCOLM E. JEWELL

Acknowledgments

A lucky author receives assistance from numerous sources. I am most deeply indebted to Malcolm Jewell for his support, encouragement, and comments on this project. Donald Gross also provided invaluable aid on earlier drafts of this manuscript. I would like to thank Paul Kleppner for his comments. I am in debt to Laura Laughlin, the director of publications at the Social Science Research Institute at Northern Illinois University, for editing the manuscript and for generating the graphics.

I would like to thank the legislative leaders and staff who discussed with me the practices of their legislative party caucus and leadership campaign committees. I am also indebted to Jeffrey Stonecash for providing data on the New York legislative caucus campaign committees.

Introduction

A relatively new development in legislative and party politics is the emergence of the legislative party as an important actor in elections in the form of caucus campaign committees and leadership campaign committees, or leadership PACs. Legislative caucus campaign committees are, as the name implies, committees of the legislative party caucus that are given the responsibility of raising funds and providing assistance to the party's legislative candidates. Leadership campaign committees are used by individual legislators to distribute funds to other legislative candidates. The involvement of these organizations in legislative elections is a development that should generate a great deal of interest among political scientists and political observers, not only because it is new, but also because of the major normative and practical implications such a development holds for party politics, legislative elections, and legislative behavior.

Because legislative party involvement in elections is relatively new, many questions have yet to be answered, including questions of origin and purpose, behavior, and effect. Why did the legislative party become involved in campaigns for legislative seats? What type of organizations are the legislative party campaign committees? Can they be considered party organizations or are they merely political action committees? What exactly are they doing? To whom are they providing campaign assistance, with what, and how much? And what effect are they having on legislative elections, legislative behavior, and party politics?

The answers to these questions have far-ranging implications for legislative politics and political parties. For instance, if legislative party campaign committees can be considered party organizations, their existence changes the structure of party organization as we know it. Legislative party committees will have to be included in any delineation of the structure of party organizations, and the characterization of the party-in-government as a component of party organizations concerned mainly with governing will have to be altered to incorporate this new electoral role. Moreover, if these committees are indeed party organizations, then they represent a party response to growing needs of legislative candidates and the increased competition for legislative seats, providing evidence of political parties' ability to adapt to the candidate-centered campaigns that typify current elections.

In terms of legislative elections and behavior, if legislative party campaign committees utilize their resources strategically, they can have a significant impact on legislative elections. If they have an influence in elections, they may also affect the behavior of legislators. For example, legislators may vote along party lines more frequently as a consequence of the assistance they receive from their party's caucus campaign committee. Moreover, as candidates' dependence on interest group contributions is decreased by the campaign resources legislative parties provide, the influence these special interests exert over lawmaking should also decline. Finally, if legislative party campaign committees concentrate their resources on marginal races and make them more competitive, the result would be an increase in representation and responsiveness, thus making legislative elections more democratic.

Thanks to work of scholars such as Paul Herrnson, Gary Jacobson, and David Adamany, a great deal is known about the activities of the legislative caucus campaign committees at the national level—the Democratic Congressional Campaign Committee (DCCC), the Democratic Senatorial Campaign Committee (DSCC), the Republican National Congressional Committee (RNCC), and the Republican National Senatorial Committee (RNSC).[1] The congressional campaign committees, which are now an integral part of the national party organization, were all very active by 1980. The Republican congressional campaign committees began their independent collection of campaign funds in 1976-77; the Democratic committees, on the other hand, did not collect a significant number of funds until the 1980s.[2] Both arose from the void in congressional elections left by the national committees, which lacked the resources needed to concentrate seriously on congressional elections.

Researchers investigating the congressional campaign committees have found that they, among other things, focus their resources
on marginal races; recruit candidates; provide services such as polling, media facilities, campaign consultants, and fund-raising; intro-
duce candidates to major contributors; and provide a mark of
legitimacy to challengers, helping them raise funds from individuals
and PACs.[3] Although the reported value of their assistance still represents only approximately 10 percent of all funds raised in congressional elections, the undervaluation of in-kind assistance, the use of
"soft money," and the fact that the committees influence the contribution decisions of other major contributors means that these committees have come to play a key role in congressional elections.
Herrnson reported that this is reflected in attitudes of congressional
candidates and staff.[4]

Unfortunately, our knowledge of legislative party campaign committees and where they fit into our party system is incomplete because very little is known about the legislative party campaign
committees at the level of state politics. Other than Malcolm Jewell's
work, which brought the existence of legislative party campaign committees at the state level to our attention, most of the work is focused
on a single state and/or deals exclusively with the distribution of campaign committee funds.[5] These works provide some evidence that
legislative party campaign committees concentrate their resources in
competitive elections, and they offer bits of evidence suggesting that
the committees may vary their strategies over time in accordance with
partisan trends. They do not, however, provide us with any picture of
what these committees are like in terms of organizational structure
and practices, and they lack the comparative and theoretical approach
necessary to make firm conclusions about the practices of legislative
party campaign committees.

The purpose of this book is to report on research that was designed to expand our knowledge of the electoral activity of legislative
parties by focusing on legislative party campaign committees at the
state level. The research consists of a comparative study of legislative
party campaign activity, with empirical analyses of campaign finance
data in ten states and qualitative analysis of interviews conducted
with legislative leaders and key staff on legislative caucus campaign
committees in eleven states. The results lead to a number of important findings regarding the organization, practices, and behavior of
legislative party campaign committees. The findings suggest that, in
the services they provide and the way they distribute their resources,

most legislative party caucus campaign committees have developed into organizations that are more akin to political parties than to PACs. Leadership PACs, on the other hand, resemble political action committees, but the way they distribute their funds, more often than not, counters the effect of PAC contributions. Such conclusions obviously have major implications for the study of legislative politics.

This book is organized so that the major questions of interest regarding the legislative party campaign committees are addressed in separate chapters. Chapter 1 examines the context in which legislative party campaign committees developed—the history of legislative elections and the role played by political parties throughout that history—in order to arrive at some understanding of why and how legislative parties became involved in elections. Chapter 2 develops a theoretical framework for the comparative study of the involvement of legislative parties in elections. The framework focuses the research and provides specific assumptions for the development of testable hypotheses; such an approach has been conspicuously absent in the literature on campaign committees. Chapter 3 provides an analysis of the finances of legislative party campaign committees at the aggregate level, allowing for some state-to-state comparisons and an initial look at the distribution of resources. The qualitative analysis of interviews begins in chapter 4, where the results of the interviews are used to determine what these committees are like: the organizational structure of caucus committees, the assistance they provide candidates, where they get their resources, and the functions that they perform. Chapter 5 looks at the actual distribution of caucus committee and leadership campaign committee resources in terms of the marginality of the race and the types of candidates supported i.e., incumbents and nonincumbents. The differences between caucus committees and leadership PACs are explored in the chapter 6. Chapter 7 explores the question of refined strategies that take into consideration the legislative party's status in the legislature and national and state party trends. The conclusion provides a discussion of the implications of the findings and offers a look into the future.

1

Legislative Elections and Political Parties

A suitable starting place for this inquiry is an examination of the factors that may have inspired legislative parties to become involved in elections. The reasons for the development of legislative party campaign committees are evident in the recent history of legislative elections. Changes such as the decline in party loyalty, the phenomenal increase in the cost of campaigns, and the increase in party competition for control of state legislatures generated a demand for assistance that only a political party organization could provide. The state and national central party organizations, as well as the local party organizations, were in no position to help, having never fully recovered from the impact of the progressive reforms and the changes that occurred in the nature of political campaigns. It is in this environment that legislative caucus campaign committees emerged, and it seems apparent that the reason they emerged was to fill this void. In fact, this was a common theme among many of the legislators and staff who were interviewed for this research. Senator Charles Pray, president of the Maine Senate, for example, stated that the Democratic Senate Caucus Committee was "started in 1978 because we were getting very little help from the party." Mark Ausmus of the House Democratic Campaign Committee in Missouri indicated that in the 1980s the Democrats "didn't have a strong state party," and that was the "reason why the speaker started it [the HDCC]."

The reason for the development of leadership PACs can be found in the increasing amount of money in legislative campaigns and, more important, in the unequal distribution of that money. PACs and individuals tend to contribute more to incumbent candidates who are most likely to win.[1] This leaves incumbent legislators, especially lead-ers who attract the most contributions because of their positions of power, with excess funds. Not having to worry too much about re-election, these leaders began to use the money to pursue other goals, namely, to advance their careers in terms of party and legislative lead-ership positions. The best way to pursue these goals was to make campaign contributions to other candidates. Such contributions, or transfers, could help the legislators advance their careers by adding to their party's chance of holding a majority of seats and by establishing a group of friends in the legislature that could provide votes in lead-ership races.

Legislative Elections

It is no exaggeration to say that political scientists' knowledge of leg-islative elections is based almost entirely on research dealing with congressional elections. The nature of state legislative elections has been largely inferred from the studies at the national level. We lack a large body of literature on state legislative elections because data on state legislative contests have not been very accessible—there are few or no survey data on the subject and only now that the State Legis-lative Election Returns data set has been compiled for the Inter-university Consortium for Political and Social Research is the basic information on election returns available for a large number of states.[2]

It is conventional wisdom that legislative elections are character-ized by a low level of voter information, low voter turnout, and high levels of incumbency reelection, and are often shaped by national and/or statewide partisan trends.[3] Because of the low levels of voter information, partisan identification undoubtedly plays a large role in voter choice, acting as a cue to the candidate's general issue positions. The high rate of incumbency is probably related to a large differential in the name recognition of incumbents versus challengers and the fact that the districts are most often relatively small and consequently ho-mogeneous. The level of professionalism in state legislatures has in-creased, making legislative seats more desirable, a development that may be reflected in the decline in legislative turnover since the 1960s.[4]

These characteristics of legislative elections, especially the low levels of information, mean that money can play a significant role in legislative contests. Money allows candidates, either little recognized incumbents or unknown nonincumbents, to fill in the void in voters' information about their candidacy. A state legislative candidate without the funds to obtain some recognition will not go far. Studies of money in legislative elections have shown that it plays an important role in the outcomes of those elections.[5] Most of these studies of legislative elections, however, have found that, although money does affect the outcome, its role is subordinate to other factors such as partisan strength in the district or the incumbency advantage.[6]

The Party Role

The role played by political parties in the election of legislative candidates has changed dramatically over the years. In the heyday of the political machines, the parties slated the candidates and provided the resources necessary to win—mainly in the form of local party cadres that mobilized the party's voters. The parties controlled the candidates and to a great extent the elections.[7] The extent of party control during this era can be illustrated by the experience of my own grandfather, a precinct captain in Chicago's Democratic organization, who ran for a seat in the Illinois legislature under the instruction of his employers (he held a patronage position). After he won, he resigned—also under instruction of his employers—so the Democratic machine could install their man, whom they obviously felt could not win an election.

The reforms enacted as a result of the progressive movement in the early 1900s initiated changes in electoral procedures that eventually minimized party involvement in legislative elections. The growth of the direct primary as the method for nominating party candidates ended the parties' role in directly selecting candidates. And the overall weakening of the political party organizations—the loss of patronage, the rise of candidate-centered campaigns for national and statewide offices, the push toward nonpartisan local elections, and the growth of the welfare state—left the parties without much life and with few resources to devote to any campaign.

To win a legislative seat candidates therefore found it necessary to create and maintain their own organizations, to obtain the necessary resources on their own, and to run their campaigns independent of party help. This candidate-centered form of politics, which came to dominance in the 1960s and 1970s, moved the political parties even further toward the fringes of the legislative electoral process. Candidates developed their own organizations in order to win the primary election, then they maintained these organizations in order to win the general election. This development, along with the decline in party loyalty among the electorate, led many political scientists and political observers to predict the eventual demise of political parties.[8]

Political parties, however, did not disappear. In fact the parties appear to be on the rebound. Their organizational strength has increased, and the national central committees have come to life with the infusion of large sums of money collected via direct mail.[9] Even with this revitalization, the national and most state central party committees did not have the resources required to become deeply involved in legislative elections, consequently it was left to the legislative parties to do so.

The Cost of Campaigns

Early in the era of candidate-centered campaigns, the effort needed to be elected or reelected was not beyond the capacity of individual candidates' organizations. The costs of campaigns were not unreasonable and candidates could always rely on the partisan base of their district for support. This changed with the introduction of new and more expensive campaign technologies such as campaign consultants, electronic media, and public opinion polling. Such measures were so effective that candidates who did not use them would be at a great disadvantage. Thus, the demand for campaign revenues to pay for these new technologies increased dramatically.

Starting in the 1970s the cost of legislative campaigns at the state and national level increased dramatically. Figure 1-1 shows that the average cost of legislative campaigns for state legislative races in a number of states and U.S. Congressional races—included for the sake of comparison—has increased tremendously since the early 1970s. Table 1-1 illustrates the enormous change in the total expenditures in these races between 1978 and 1986. Total expenditures in Oregon senate races increased 379.1 percent; in California assembly races, expenditures rose 144.8 percent; while expenditures for U.S. House races and U.S. Senate races increased "only" 144.5 percent and 183.4 percent respectively.[10] This occurred in a period of less than ten years! The escalating costs of campaigns even outpaced inflation in all but one state.[11]

In addition to the cost of new campaign technologies, this growth in campaign financing was fueled, in part, by the rapid increase in the

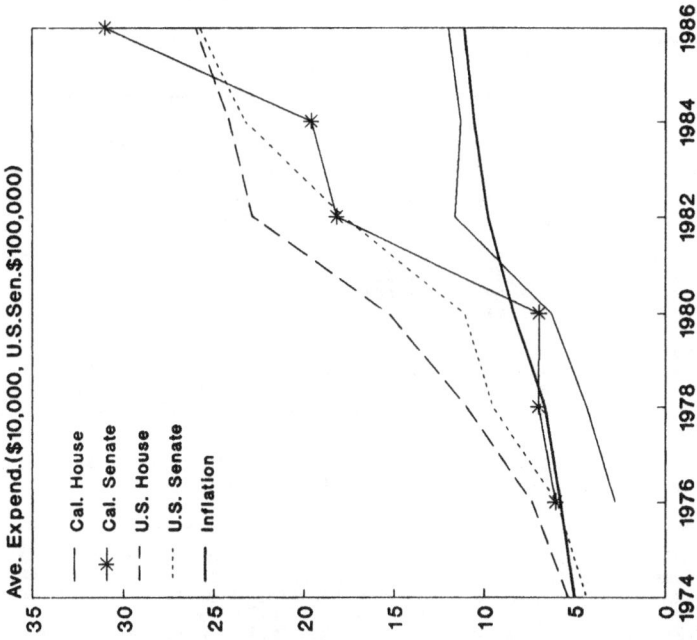

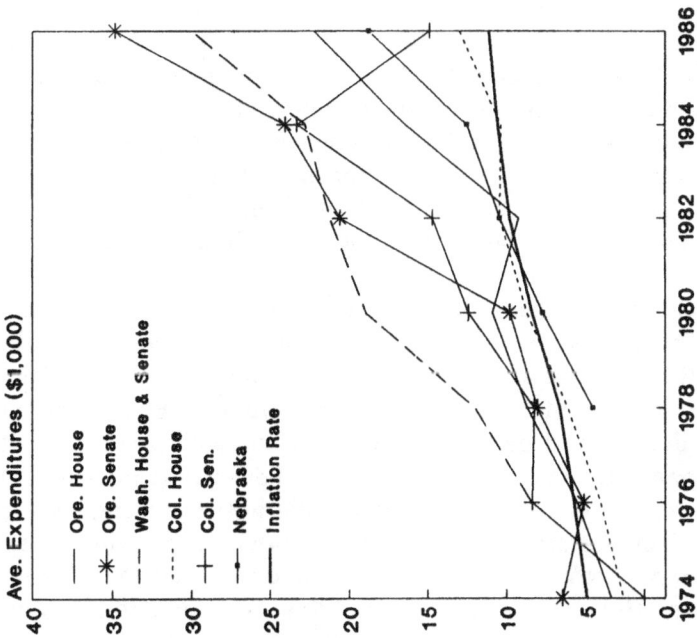

Figure 1-1. Average Campaign Expenditures in Legislative Elections

Table 1-1. Trends in Campaign Finance

			Total Expenditures	
	1978	1986	% increase 1978-1986	% increase in 1978 dollars
U.S. House Races	$86,129,169	210,626,146	144.5%	19.9%
U.S. Senate Races	64,595,510	183,039,105	183.4	38.9
State House Races				
California	7,485,837	18,322,538	144.8	20.0
Colorado	798,255	1,684,826	111.1	3.5
Oregon	1,013,711	2,577,216	154.2	24.7
State Senate Races				
California	3,134,451	12,095,060	285.9	89.2
Colorado	279,912	505,642	80.6	-11.4
Oregon	225,265	1,079,299	379.1	134.9
Nebraska	360,884	1,470,650	307.5	99.8
Washington H & S	2,790,000	6,970,000	149.8	22.5

Sources: Ornstein et al., Vital Statistics on Congress 1987-1988, 1987. California Fair Political Practices Commission, 1986 General Election: Campaign Receipts and Expenditures, July 1, 1986 through December 31, 1986, 1987. Colorado Secretary of State, Elections, 1986 Colorado Campaign Reform Act Summary: Contributions and Expenditures, Nebraska Accountability and Disclosure Commission, A Summary of Political Campaign Financing: The Candidates, 1986. Oregon Secretary of State, Elections Division, Summary Report of Campaign Contributions and Expenditures: 1986 General Election. Washington Public Disclosure Commission, 1986 Election Financing Fact Book.

number of political action committees at the national level following the Federal Election Campaign Act of 1974. This growth explosion quickly caught on at the state level.[12] Contributions from individuals and PACs, however, tend to go largely to incumbent candidates who are relatively safe.[13] This resulted in more money in campaigns but proportionately less money for nonincumbents—open-seat candidates and challengers—and unestablished incumbents. In other words, it compounded the problem of the high cost of campaigns rather than helping to solve it.

The need for large sums of money in order to run for or hold onto a legislative seat places an enormous burden on legislative candidates. As the executive director of the Illinois House Republican Campaign Committee put it, "some seats are up around a hundred thousand dollars, and districts do not have the ability to raise that kind of money." It has meant that legislators have had to increase the time they devote to fund-raising activities. Because the rising level of professionalism in state legislatures has increased the time that a legislator's job requires, it is probably even harder to find the time for fund-raising. Thus, by the mid- to late 1970s, there existed a heightened demand for another source of campaign funds, one that would not consume any more of a legislator's time and one that could channel the funds to candidates who needed them the most.

The Rise of Insecurity in Legislative Elections

The 1960s and 1970s also witnessed a decline in partisan loyalty among the electorate. The percentage of the population identifying with either of the major parties declined, and the number of people splitting their votes between the two parties increased dramatically.[14] The waning party loyalty of the electorate added an additional element of uncertainty to legislative elections: no longer could a candidate depend on a large loyal partisan base.[15] In other words, the increase in "swing" voters in the districts' electorates opened up legislative elections to other influences. Thus, weakened party ties translated into an increased potential for competition for a legislative seat, because district party strength was no longer the barrier to a serious challenge that it used to be.[16]

Since the 1950s, the margin of seats held by majority parties in state legislatures has declined. Figure 1-2 shows the margin of party control in state houses in four regions since 1950, measured in terms of the difference between the percentage of seats held by the majority party and by the minority party. In the South, Midwest, and Northeast there has been a decline in the difference in the percentage of seats held by the majority.[17] The slopes of the lines are -.260 for the Northeast, -.448 for the Midwest, -.561 for the South, and .002 for the West. All but the slope for the west were significant at a .01 level. The decrease in legislative margins indicates an increase in competition for control of state legislatures and, consequently, a threat to the majority party's control. These trends mean that the 1960s and 1970s were not only an era of increased insecurity for the individual legislative candidates but also were a time of increased insecurity for legislative parties.

The Emergence of Legislative Party Campaign Committees

By the mid- to late 1970s, the increasing cost of campaigns and the added uncertainty about reelection—two developments that are undoubtedly strongly interrelated—meant that legislative candidates

Margin (Marjority seats-Minority seats)

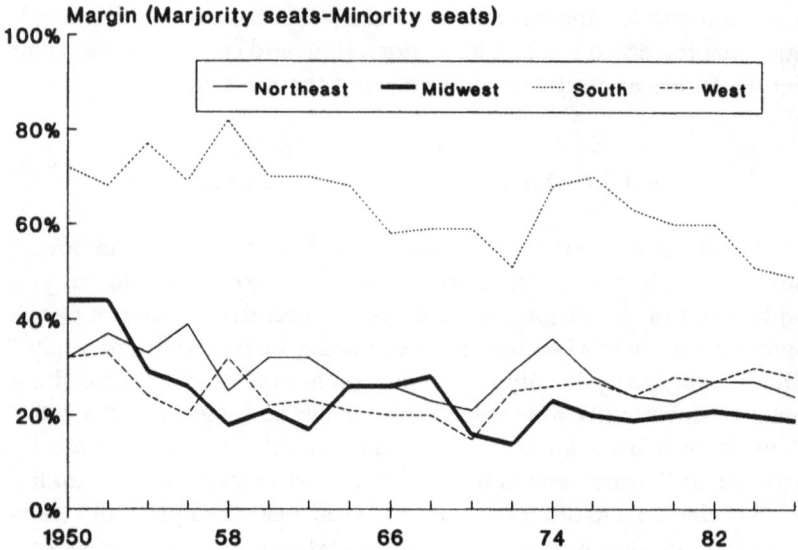

Figure 1-2. Margin of Party Control in State Houses

needed additional assistance for their campaigns. The increase in competition for control of the legislature denoted an increase in insecurity for the legislative party as well. For the individual candidate, plenty of PAC money was available, but most of it was being distributed to incumbent candidates, who were relatively safe.[18] There was a need for a centralized organization to provide assistance to candidates based upon need and to protect the interests of the party within the legislature; in other words, the demand was for a political party organization. Central committees of most state and national party organizations, however, could not meet this demand, consequently leaving a void.

The widespread existence today of legislative party campaign committees at the national and state levels is undoubtedly a result of the need to fill that void. Legislative party caucus campaign committees represent a centralized source of campaign funds that candidates in need can go to for assistance. In addition to providing cash, the caucus campaign committees purchase some of the expensive campaign technologies—polling, media production facilities, and campaign consultants—at volume discounts and pass those discounts on to their candidates. Furthermore, caucus campaign committees provide the legislative party with the mechanism for maintaining or pursuing a legislative majority. Leadership PACs represent the redistribution of campaign funds from the "wealthy" to the "needy" candidates, an arrangement that benefits both the recipient and the contributor.

The extent to which legislative caucus campaign committees exist in the American states is presented in Table 1-2. The pattern of regional differences is most apparent. The region where such committees seem least likely to exist is the South. Legislative elections in the South are still dominated by the Democratic party, with most legislative elections remaining uncontested, so that there is little need for legislative party campaign committees to protect the interests either of insecure individuals or of the legislative parties.[19] In the sample of states used in this book the strongest caucus campaign committees tend to be found in states with high levels of party competition and high campaign expenditures, or with weak state party organizations. The best developed caucus campaign committees within each state tend to be Democratic committees—such as those in Wisconsin, Maine, Minnesota, and Indiana. This may have something to do with the fact that the Democratic state party organizations in those states tend to be weaker than the Republican state party organizations.[20]

Legislative leadership campaign committees (leadership PACs) undoubtedly have their roots in the unequal distribution of campaign contributions. Candidates who have funds and do not need them have found that campaign money can be used to advance their careers in the legislature.[21] Consequently, these candidates have developed the practice of transferring funds out of their own campaign committees to the campaign committees of candidates who need them. In the process they build friendships that will support them in future bids for leadership positions. Thus, leadership PACs developed almost entirely because of the enormous increases in the amount of money involved in legislative elections and the unequal distribution of that money. They developed for different reasons than the caucus campaign committees, and this is indicated by the fact that they coexist with caucus committees in every state in the eleven-state sample used in this analysis.

In summary, an examination of the context in which legislative party campaign committees developed provides reasonable explanations as to why the legislative party became involved in legislative elections. The growth in the costs of campaigns, the increased competition for control of legislatures, and the weakness of state and national central party organizations created a need for political parties

Table 1-2. States with Legislative Caucus Campaign Committees

	Yes	No		Yes	No
Northeast					
Connecticut	x		Vermont	NA**	
New Hampshire		x	New Jersey	x	
Maine*	x		New York*	x	
Massachusetts	x		Pennsylvania	x	
Rhode Island	x				
Midwest					
Illinois*	x		Kansas	x	
Indiana*	x		Minnesota*	x	
Michigan	x		Nebraska		x
Ohio	x		North Dakota		x
Wisconsin*	x		South Dakota	x	
Iowa		x			
South					
Delaware	x		Kentucky		x
Florida	x		Mississippi		x
Georgia	NA		Tennessee*	x	
Maryland		x	Arkansas	x	
North Carolina	x		Louisiana	NA	
South Carolina		x	Oklahoma	x	
Virginia	x		Missouri*	x	
West Virginia	x		Texas	x	
Alabama		x			
West					
Arizona		x	Utah	x	
Colorado		x	Wyoming		x
California*	x		Alaska	x	
Idaho	x		Hawaii	x	
Montana	x		Oregon*	x	
Nevada	x		Washington*	x	
New Mexico	x				

*Indicates states used for analysis in the rest of the book.

**NA indicates information was not available.

in legislative elections. Out of this need grew the legislative caucus campaign committees. Leadership PACs developed at a time when a large amount of funding was being placed in the hands of those who did not need it for reelection.

2
Theory and Method

What are legislative party campaign committees like? Are they party organizations or merely party PACs? What strategies do legislative party campaign committees pursue? Do they merely support their own—incumbent candidates—or are they more inclusive? How do legislative party campaign committees differ from each other? Do leadership PACs and caucus campaign committees differ beyond their organizational structures? Such questions represent the main purpose of this research because of the implications the answers hold for legislative elections, political parties, and legislative behavior. In order to answer these questions it is necessary to form some a priori expectations about what the answers might be: this is done by generating hypotheses from a theory of legislative party campaign committee behavior. The purpose of this chapter is to develop some a priori expectations about legislative party campaign committees and to discuss the data and methods that will be used to determine whether or not legislative party campaign committees conform to those expectations.

Constrained Rational Decision Making: A Theoretical Framework

Two general theoretical approaches have been used in the campaign finance literature: the rational choice approach and the organizational perspective.[1] The rational choice approach assumes that actors involved in financing campaigns are rational decision makers who act to maximize the benefit they derive from the contributions they make. Welch's work provides one example of this approach.[2] Welch argued that there were two types of contributors, quid pro quo and ideological, both of whom he portrayed as rational. The quid pro quo contributor expects returns from his or her contribution, in terms of favorable policy, etc. Since the best returns come from investing in those who will wield power, quid pro quo contributors give overwhelmingly to incumbents.[3]

The organizational approach argues that organizational variables—such as the decision-making structure—determine how decisions will be made. This was demonstrated by Herrnson, who found that the Democratic Congressional Campaign Committee's (DCCC) decisions were affected by the power that incumbent Democratic congressmen had over the committee. The incumbent Democrats used their power over the committee to obtain additional campaign contributions from the committee, consequently limiting the DCCC's ability to strategically target resources to close races.[4]

Unlike many other competing theories in political science, these two approaches are quite compatible.[5] The validity of one does not rule out the validity of the other. In more concrete terms, it is possible, if not entirely likely, that rational decision making can exist within the limitations set by organizational or environmental factors. In fact, to hold the decision maker to an ideal of rational decision making without considering such external constraints sacrifices too much realism for the sake of a parsimonious theory of decision making.[6]

Integrating these two approaches to studying campaign finance will provide the basic theoretical framework used in this research. I posit that legislative party campaign committee behavior can be understood and explained within the context of three components of the theory: (1) the assumption that the actors involved are rational decision makers, (2) the proposition that the actors have discernible goal structures related to legislative party campaign committee behavior, and (3) the proposition that organizational factors affect the choices made by the legislative party campaign committees.

The Assumption of Rationality. The cornerstone of this theoretical framework is the assumption that the legislators—the actors involved in legislative party campaign committee decisions—behave rationally. That legislators are rational decision makers in this case simply means that their behavior is goal oriented. Legislators are assumed to have a clear set of goals, and their behavior should follow the pattern of maximizing outcomes in terms of these goals, while minimizing costs. Understanding legislative party campaign committee activity should, therefore, follow from an understanding of the goals of those involved.

Assumptions regarding the rationality of decision makers are grounded in rational choice theory. Rational choice theorists have been criticized for their tendency to make demanding assumptions and to oversimplify the choice process in the "real world." Their critics argue that their models often ignore important constraints on time, information, and human mental capacities and that, instead of rationally maximizing their utility, decision makers "muddle through" incrementally, or "satisfice."[7]

Because this research borrows from rational choice theory, the possibility that it may be open to some of the same criticisms must be addressed. These criticisms are not especially relevant to this research for a number of reasons. First, this research is not designed to "test" the assertion that decision makers are rational per se. That assumption is simply being used as a heuristic device to organize and to integrate the theoretical development and to provide a framework for the generation of testable hypotheses and the interpretation of findings. Second, this research is dealing with political elites, who are more likely than nonelites to meet the stringent requirements of the rational model; they are more likely than nonelites to have clear, prioritized goals and sufficient information, and they are more likely to select options that will lead to their goals. Thus, the limits on individual rationality should not pose a problem for this research.[8]

Using rational choice assumptions in research is not something entirely new to political science. Political scientists have used the framework of rational choice theory to develop theories on a large number of subjects but the rational choice assumptions seem to have been more readily accepted when used for constructing theories of elite behavior.[9] The assumption of rational decision making has provided the basis for theories regarding electoral strategies, political parties, and legislative behavior—three aspects of legislative party campaign finance activity of concern in this research.[10]

Goals: Legislators, Leaders, and Parties.   In the legislature there are three types of actors especially relevant to the study of legislative party campaign committees: individual legislators, the legislative leaders, and the legislative political parties. Each set of actors can be seen as having a particular goal structure related to the activity of legislative party campaign committees.

Legislators' primary goal is to be reelected.[11] They can be expected to amass as many resources as necessary and possible to attain this goal, for if they are not reelected, nothing else matters. Fenno argued that, beyond reelection, legislators pursue the goals of power and influence in the legislature and of "good" public policy, i.e., the legislation they wish to see enacted.[12] Power and influence in the legislature may include obtaining a assignment, or even a chair position, on a powerful or important committee. The chances of obtaining the goals of power and influence and "good" public policy are tied to the status of the legislator's party. Majority party legislators will have a greater opportunity to attain their goals.

The goal structure of the legislative leadership is likely to be more complex because their goals encompass collective party goals as well as individual goals. Leaders, like all legislators, are likely to pursue the individual goal of reelection to the legislature. In addition, because of their party leadership positions, they may also pursue a number of other goals such as, reelection to their leadership posts, majority status for their parties, large personal coalitions, and party cohesion. Leaders are likely to value majority status for their parties because of the benefits they derive from being the majority leader or Speaker: power over committee appointments, scheduling of legislation, and the ability to enact desired policies, to name a few. Benefits derived from being the minority leader are significantly less. Leaders are also likely to pursue large personal coalitions to provide themselves with the power base needed to retain their leadership positions. Leaders should value party cohesion because it enhances their power within the legislature as well as their power within the party. Party cohesion makes leaders' jobs easier.

Two goals held by those in leadership positions—majority party status and party cohesion—are shared by the political party and thus may be considered more collective in nature than the personal or individual goals of reelection (to the legislature and to the leadership post) and building a personal coalition. The relative emphasis placed upon the goals shared with the party as compared with the more individual goals should depend in part upon the level of party competition within the state. High levels of party competition mean a greater uncertainty about what the partisan makeup of the legislature will be after an election. Such uncertainty should prompt leaders to devote a great deal of energy and resources to electing a majority of their party, after they insure their own reelection, of course. After leaders devote the resources deemed necessary to win majority status, then they may use whatever additional resources are needed to pursue the goals of a large personal coalition, party cohesion, and policy enactment. Under low levels of party competition, the uncertainty regarding the party's status in the legislature is reduced, allowing leaders to pursue more personal goals.

When determining the likely goals of the legislative party, care must be taken regarding the assumption of rationality for a collective body. Rational choice theory deals with individual preferences and choices and argues that collective action is deduced from these individual processes. A collective rational calculus cannot be assumed because a collective utility function cannot be determined because of intrasitivities that occur when aggregeting individuals' preferences.[13] Thus, a collective body is expected to be no more than the summation of the goals and choices of the individuals who constitute it. Downs's definition of a political party as a coalition of individuals who have certain ends in common and who cooperate to achieve them conforms to this rational perspective of collective action.[14] Thus, under the assumptions of rational choice theory, the legislative party goal structure should reflect the goals and choices of its members, and a legislative party campaign committee should not be construed to be an individual entity with goals and purposes of its own.[15]

In contrast to this rational choice view is the notion found in organizational theory that bureaucratic organizations can, and most often do, become separate entities distinct from the individuals who comprise them.[16] Furthermore, organizational theorists argue that bureaucratic organizations do have goals and purposes of their own that are distinct from those of the individuals who make up the organizations. However, the rational choice assumption that a separate "collective rationality" does not exist is not likely to be contradicted in this analysis because legislative party campaign committees are unlikely to be considered full-blown bureaucratic organizations. That is, they do not have the hierarchical structure, specialization of tasks, technically trained personnel, and standardized operating procedures characteristic of bureaucratic organizations. Organizational factors obviously have an impact on legislative party campaign committee behavior, but the underlying assumption for the purpose of this research remains individual rationality.

Because it is assumed that the legislative party's goals stem from the goals of its individual members, the goals of the legislative party must reflect those of the legislators and the legislative leaders. This is easier to demonstrate in the case of leaders than in the case of individual legislators. I posit that the goals of the legislative party are (1) majority party status and a maximum number of seats, (2) party cohesion, and (3) the enactment of party policies.

The extent to which the goals of those who occupy leadership positions are entangled with the legislative party goals has already been discussed. Leaders value majority party status highly because being majority leader results in much greater benefits than being minority leader. Leaders also value party cohesion because it enhances their power within the legislature and within the party and because it makes their jobs easier. Thus, the legislative party's goals presented above easily reflect the goals of the leaders.

It is a little harder to show how the legislative party's goals reflect the goals of individual legislators. The difficulty arises from the classic dilemma between collective and individual goals. By pursuing a strategy of maximizing seats, the legislative party cannot guarantee that each individual legislator will be reelected—legislators' primary and dominant goal. In fact, the most efficient distribution of resources to maximize seats will concentrate on races perceived to be close, a strategy that leaves many incumbent legislators without assistance. Though they may have won by large margins in past elections and may be perceived to have safe seats, legislators always worry about reelection[17] and thus prefer that they receive the legislative party's money.[18] However, the party's goal of maximizing seats to gain majority status does reflect the goals of some of its members, specifically those legislators in competitive races who would receive assistance. Furthermore, legislators in "safe" seats may consider the future value that a party that pursues seat-maximizing goals might bring them if they were ever in a close race. They may support it as a type of "insurance" policy that they can collect from if they run into electoral trouble.[19] Thus, in certain instances the party's goals do reflect the reelection goal of legislators.

Individual legislators' goals of power and influence in the legislature and of "good" public policy are easily reflected in the party goals of majority status, party cohesion, and policy enactment. Majority party status enhances the legislators' power in terms of committee assignments and increases the likelihood that legislation legislators favor will be enacted. This leads us to a conclusion about party goals that fits closely with the literature.

In summary, the goal structures of those involved in legislative party campaign committees differ mainly in regard to the difference between collective and individual goals. Nonetheless, the proposed goal structures are quite similar since a number of the individual goals depend upon the attainment of many of the collective goals; for example, the majority leader's status depends upon the party's ability to meet its goal of a majority of seats. This tie between collective and individual goals is greatest when the collective goals are threatened, which occurs under high levels of interparty competition. High levels of interparty competition increase the likelihood that legislators may end up in the minority, depriving the legislators of the committee assignments and policy outcomes they desire. The similarities and differences between the goals of the various actors will play a key part in the explanation and prediction of legislative party campaign committee behavior.

Organizational Factors.   The organizational structure and resources of legislative party campaign committees determine whose goals the committees pursue as well as which goals they can pursue. The decision-making structure of the committees—who makes the decisions—will affect the committees' behavior by determining whose goals will be pursued. For instance, if a leader controls the committee, the committee will pursue the leader's goals—majority party status, a personal coalition, and so on. Committees controlled by incumbent legislators will pursue the goals of the incumbents, mainly helping them get reelected. If pure party interests are in control—in other words, if no candidate has a voice—then the party goals of majority party status and party cohesion will be pursued.[20] The effect of the decision-making structure on legislative party campaign committee behavior is likely to be the most obvious when comparing legislative caucus campaign committees and leadership campaign committees. The former is controlled by the caucus members or the leadership, the latter by a single legislator.

The second organizational factor that is believed to shape legislative party campaign committee decisions is the amount of resources available. Legislative party campaign committees have limited resources for legislative campaigns, especially when compared to the contributions from individuals and from political action committees. California legislative party campaign committees, the wealthiest in the nation, make up about a quarter of the funds raised by candidates in legislative elections; other states are far behind (see chapter 3). Because resources are limited, a widespread distribution of resources would result in only token payments to individuals. Such a distribution would have limited utility for both the recipient and the contributor. Thus, the limited amount of funds possessed by the committees means they are restricted in which goals they can effectively pursue; they cannot effectively pursue goals that require a broad distribution of resources.

Finally, legislative party campaign committees' actions may be limited by campaign finance laws. States vary greatly in how they treat campaign committees, ranging from a total prohibition of such committees—in California, caucus and leadership campaign committees have now been banned as the result of a voter initiative, Proposition 73—to simply requiring that the committees file reports of revenues and expenditures. Some states have public financing and accompanying limits on contributions. Whatever the state provisions are, they can have major impact on how the committees operate by limiting how effectively the committees can pursue the goals of those involved.

In summary, the theoretical framework assumes that the actors involved are rational, argues that the actors have particular sets of goals, and contends that organizational factors play a role in determining which goals will be pursued by the committees. Goals predict the behavior of rational decision makers, and the organizational factors determine or limit which goals will be pursued. So, for example, if legislators control the campaign committee, the committee can be expected to exhibit behavior that is most effective at attaining the goals of reelecting the legislators, enhancing their power, and enacting desired legislation, all within the limits of the resources available to the committee. This framework now allows us to develop some more specific a priori expectations regarding legislative party campaign committees.

Hypotheses

Given the theoretical framework and the previous research on legislative party campaign committees, what results can be expected in an analysis of legislative party campaign committees? That is, what are the committees expected to be like? How should they be allocating their resources? And what differences should there be in the practices between legislative caucus campaign committees and leadership campaign committees?

Close Races, Nonincumbents, and the Difference Between Committees. A key component of the theory previously outlined is that the goals that legislative party campaign committees pursue are strongly related to their behavior. Legislative party campaign committees may pursue the goals of individual legislators, legislative leaders, or the collective goals of the party. Which they pursue depends upon the level of influence that legislators and leaders have over committee decision making and what their resources will allow them to do. That is, the goals that are pursued by the legislative party campaign committee will be determined in part by the organizational structure.

If the legislative party campaign committees pursue the legislators' goals, how will they distribute their resources? Conventional wisdom, as well as rational choice research on distributional politics,[21] leads us to believe that where reelection-valuable resources are concerned, incumbent legislators will fight for and win their fair share of whatever the committees distribute. In fact, according to Shepsle and Weingast, the fear of being in the minority and losing out on resources valuable for reelection should lead to a norm of universalism among legislators, a situation where every legislator receives a share.[22] However, the fact that legislative party campaign committees have limited resources narrows their options. As a result, they may either distribute token amounts to all caucus members or target close races—including nonincumbent candidates—in order to build or maintain a legislative majority.

Because the game of legislative elections is one of repetition, at least for most players, legislators should opt for the second strategy of targeting resources. There are two reasons to expect this. First, safe incumbents should be willing to pay the cost of forgoing the token benefit at the present time in exchange for the greater benefit they would accrue if they were ever to face a strong challenger. In other words, with the legislative party campaign committee targeting races, the potential payoff—a concentration of campaign assistance when it is needed—is greater than the cost—the loss of a token benefit every election in which it is not needed.

Second, legislators should opt for a strategic distribution of campaign resources because the benefits derived from being in the majority party, namely, favorable committee assignments and favorable outcomes on public policy, should be greater than the benefit derived from the token amount that an equal distribution of legislative party resources would bring. In cases where the legislature is dominated by one party and the hopes or fears of a change in status are remote, this calculus would obviously be very different. Majority party status would no longer be an important goal because there is no fear of losing a majority or because attaining a majority is no longer a realistic goal. This makes the individual goal of reelection the dominant one.

Under these conditions legislative party campaign committees should be found to support only incumbents.

When analyzing the role of the legislative leaders in committee decisions, it is important to distinguish between the two types of committees: caucus campaign committees and leadership campaign committees or leadership PACs. The distributional decisions of legislative caucus campaign committees under the control of party leaders may be very different from the distributional decisions of leaders directing their own campaign committee funds. In the first capacity, leaders are in charge of the legislative party's money and thus must heed some of the demands of other party members. In the other capacity, leaders are in charge of their own funds and are therefore less constrained when making distributional decisions.

If leaders exercise control over caucus committees' decisions, it is expected that the committees will concentrate their resources on close races, whether these involve incumbents or nonincumbents. Legislative leaders have to balance the particular demands of the rank-and-file legislators of their own party and the needs of the party as a whole, because leaders' ability to reach their own goals depends upon both. Leaders' goal of maintaining or advancing their leadership position depends upon the vote of the legislators within their party and on the status of their party within the legislature. To the extent that legislators see the benefit of a concentrated allocation of resources, no conflict exists between the individual and collective goals, and the leaders are free to pursue collective party goals through a strategic allocation of the caucus committee's resources. This is most likely to occur under conditions of high party competition for control of the legislature. Also, under these conditions the need to be responsive to the party members precludes legislative party leaders from favoring their loyal followers at the expense of others.

When party competition is low, this pattern is likely to break down, causing leaders to sacrifice collective party goals in order to meet the demands of their party's legislators. Consequently, the committee's resources would be distributed equally, or only to caucus members, i.e., incumbent legislators. Low levels of party competition may also make it necessary for leaders of the majority party to defend their position if factionalism threatens it, encouraging them to distribute resources based upon personal loyalties rather than need and partisanship—a practice that would unquestionably lead to a high level of divisiveness among the party caucus members.

Since leadership PACs involve the distribution of an individual legislative leader's personal campaign funds to other candidates, the distribution of these funds should be directed at attaining the leader's goals. To a certain extent, leaders can be expected to act in a manner similar to Welch's quid pro quo contributors.[23] That is, leaders should be expected to contribute to candidates in return for the candidates' support in leadership battles. Leaders' goals, however, are tied to the fortunes of their party. If their party is constantly battling for control of the legislature, leaders' decisions about whom to support can be expected to be based upon the same criteria used by the party—i.e., the competitiveness of the race—in order to advance the goal of majority status. It is likely, though, that troubled candidates who are friends of the leader would constitute a higher priority. Under this scenario funding would go first to incumbents in trouble.

If, on the other hand, control of the legislature is unlikely to change hands, leaders' funding decisions should be based strictly on loyalty or friendship, meaning that incumbents would receive an even greater share of the available funds. This pattern is expected since, as in the logic of quid pro quo contributors, incumbents are a better investment—they are a known quantity, and they will more than likely be there following the election. To the extent that the leaders are rational, in the sense that they want to maximize the return from their expenditures, their efforts should also be expected to be devoted to those incumbents in close races where the impact per dollar will be the greatest. Whereas competitiveness should be the dominant criteria for the party, loyalty and friendship should be the dominant factor in leaders' decisions regarding their own campaign committees. This difference should result in a pattern in which leadership PACs give a greater emphasis than caucus committees to incumbent candidates.

If the legislative party campaign committees pursue the collective goals of the party, a strategic distribution of resources should also be discovered. Parties' overriding goal is to gain control of government by winning the most votes, and they do this in legislative elections by trying to win a majority of seats.[24] The most effective use of their resources to attain this goal is to concentrate the resources on races where they will make the most difference, namely, close races. Furthermore, if they are trying to build a majority, they will need to fund caucus outsiders—nonincumbent candidates—to increase the size of their party's legislative contingent. If they hold a large majority, they should be found to concentrate their resources on defending weak incumbents.

Thus, where party competition is high and resources limited, the goals of individual legislators, leaders, and the party should converge, giving priority to the shared goal of majority party status. This premise is overwhelmingly supported by the interviews conducted as part of this research. When asked, "What is the campaign committee trying to accomplish by providing assistance to candidates?" every committee representative answered that the number one goal was to gain or maintain a majority of seats in the legislature. The goals leaders pursue in distributing their own committee funds are expected to be slightly different, with a priority on supporting friends and loyal supporters. Given these goals, it is possible to devise hypotheses regarding the expected behavior of the committees and how they will differ. To gain or maintain majority party status, legislative party caucus campaign committees should be found to distribute their resources strategically, concentrating them on close races and supporting nonincumbent candidates as well as incumbents.[25] Leadership PACs also should be found to concentrate their giving to close races, but with a higher priority on incumbents, a priority that is expected to be even more distinguished if no change in the status of the leader's party is expected. Figure 2-1 depicts the expected behavior of the committees under varying conditions of party competition.

These expectations differ significantly from what one would expect following the rational choice literature on distributional politics or from conventional wisdom.[26] Both of these approaches would lead one to expect an equal distribution of campaign committee resources. The rational choice approach would lead one to expect an equal distribution because rational choice fails to take into account the organizational or environmental context of decisions—the limited resources possessed by the committees—which, to a great extent, determines which goals the committees will pursue. And conventional wisdom, assuming the complete dominance of the goal of reelection, leads to the expectation that where reelection-valuable resources are concerned, such as pork-barrel projects, legislators will fight to get their fair share, resulting in an equal distribution of committee funds limited to caucus members.

Variations in Distributional Strategies. The use of legislative party campaign committee funds to pursue the goal of majority status undoubtedly involves more than concentrating resources on close races and funding nonincumbent candidates. It is possible that the decision makers in control of legislative party campaign committees consider or make use of additional decision-making rules. Two that seem to have been in evidence in some of the literature on legislative party

Campaign Committee

	Caucus Committees	Leadership PACs
high	close races nonincumbents	close races incumbents
low	incumbents	incumbents

party competition

Figure 2-1. Expected Distribution Patterns of Campaign Committees

committees are the status of the party within the legislature—whether the party holds a majority or a minority of seats—and trends in the popularity of the party.

An efficient use of resources to attain the goal of majority party status may require more than a simple strategy of supporting candidates in competitive races. A minority party must actively recruit and support new candidates—nonincumbents—in order to increase the number of seats they hold in the legislature. This type of "offensive" strategy is the only way that they can attain majority status. Members of the legislative party caucus, according to the theoretical propositions developed above, are willing to forgo the contributions that they would receive from the committee in order to attain the goal of majority party status. Members of a minority legislative party caucus campaign committee should be even more willing to do so, because the change from minority to majority status would mean a greater payoff in terms of committee assignments and success of favored legislation. Thus, minority party legislative party campaign committees should exhibit a greater willingness to fund nonincumbent candidates. Once again, this calculus will be different for legislatures dominated by one party. Where the chances of a change in the party's status are small, the goal of majority party status is not a priority, and the willingness to allow committee funds to go to outsiders would not exist.

All a majority legislative party campaign committee has to do is to make sure that the party retains all of its legislative seats. That is, the majority party must insure that its incumbents are reelected and that the party wins any open seats created by a retirement of one of their incumbents. Since legislative incumbents are almost unbeatable at the national and state level, the most efficient way to distribute the committee's resources in order to attain the goal of majority status would be to use the resources to reinforce the incumbency advantage. Thus, majority legislative party campaign committees should follow a "defensive" strategy that puts a top priority on defending vulnerable incumbents. Unlike the minority party committees, this strategy is likely to be more prevalent as the size of the majority increases.

In attempting to gain or maintain a majority, it might also be expected that the legislative party campaign committees would take advantage of swings in party popularity to increase the number of seats the party holds. When the public's perception of the party is positive (for such reasons as having a popular candidate at the top of the ticket) campaign committees may try to "cash in" on that popularity by supporting nonincumbent candidates, and in that way increase their seats in the legislature. High popularity, it is assumed, will translate into votes. In this way a legislative party is using trends in partisan support among the public to counter the incumbency advantage.

If public perceptions of the party are negative because of such occurrences as scandal or economic downturns, campaign committees may try to counteract these trends in order to avoid losing what they already have. In other words, legislative party campaign committees whose state or national party's popularity is low should be found to focus their efforts on defending weak incumbents. In this way they make use of the incumbency advantage to try to reduce the effects of the negative changes in partisan support among the electorate.[27]

Alternatively, it is quite possible that decision makers ignore national and statewide trends when making their decisions and instead focus mainly on district-level forces such as the closeness of the previous race, the strength of the candidates, and trends in local politics.

Summary.   From the findings of previous studies and the theoretical propositions developed, a number of specific a priori expectations have been generated regarding the allocation of legislative party campaign committee resources. These expectations can be summarized in a series of hypotheses.

1. Legislative party campaign committees should be found to concentrate their resources on close races.
2. Legislative party campaign committees should be just as likely to fund nonincumbent candidates as incumbent candidates, all other factors being equal.

3. Campaign committees existing in states with low levels of interparty competition will not meet the expectations of hypothesis 2. In other words, they will not necessarily be more likely to fund nonincumbents.

4. Legislative leadership PACs should be as efficient at concentrating their resources on close races as are caucus campaign committees in states with a high degree of interparty competition.

5. Leadership PACs should be less likely than caucus campaign committees to fund nonincumbents.

6. Minority legislative party campaign committees that have a reasonable chance of winning a majority of seats should be found to concentrate a greater proportion of their resources on nonincumbent candidates than their majority party counterparts.

7. Legislative party caucus campaign committees whose parties are enjoying a surge of popularity nationally should be more likely to fund nonincumbent candidates than legislative party caucus campaign committees of the opposition.

8. Legislative party caucus campaign committees whose party is enjoying a surge of popularity at the state level should be more likely to fund nonincumbent candidates than legislative party caucus campaign committees of the opposition.

The tests of these hypotheses constitute the core of the research presented in the following chapters.

Data and Methods

The data for this research was collected from two sources. Data on the distribution of legislative party campaign committees came from various state agencies that maintain such records, and information about the organization and practices of the committees came from interviews of legislative leaders and caucus committee staff.

Most states now require that campaign finance information, including itemized revenues and expenditures for candidates, PACs and party committees, be filed with a state agency.[28] Data on legislative caucus campaign contributions were collected from ten states: California, Illinois, Indiana, Minnesota, Missouri, New York, Oregon, Tennessee, Washington, and Wisconsin.[29] Selection was based upon a number of criteria. The first criterion was the level of legislative party campaign committee activity that existed in the state. States with varying levels of legislative party campaign committee activity, either legislative party caucus campaign committees or leadership PACs, were selected. States were also selected to provide variation in types of legislative party campaign committees, namely, to include legislative caucus campaign committees and leadership campaign committees.

The campaign finance data consist of cash and in-kind contributions from caucus campaign committees and leadership PACs to individual candidates running for seats in the state house and senate for the elections of 1982, 1984, and 1986. A contribution from a leadership PAC was included if it was from a current member of the chamber for which the candidate was running. These figures are available because the states require that the candidate and party committees itemize their revenues and expenditures. Data on leadership PACs was impossible to obtain from some of the states.

A cautionary note: two potential problems exist in any study looking at state campaign finance data. First, there are differences between the states in recording campaign finances. Second, factors that vary for each state affect the level of campaign spending. States record contributions for different time periods, require revenues be itemized at different minimum levels, and have varying levels of enforcement of reporting.[30] Levels of spending can be affected by the size of the district, the availability and cost of media, the wealth of the state, campaign finance laws, and the level of competition, that is, whether or not candidates are involved in a "campaign spending arms race."

This research avoids these problems in two ways. First, the very nature of the research renders many of the differences irrelevant. We are not concerned with the relative value of campaign finance dollars from state to state, for which these problems would be very difficult to manage. Instead our interest lies in how the particular campaign committees operate in terms of the distribution of their funds. Second, any comparative analysis conducted for this research is done using the proportion of the legislative party campaign committee funds received by candidates. This provides an indication of how the committees divide their resources among candidates. Comparisons are facilitated because the analysis is not in terms of dollars.

In addition to the campaign finance data, interviews were conducted with legislative leaders or top legislative caucus staff in each of the states and the state of Maine.[31] The interviews were conducted via telephone, following the interview schedule reproduced in the appendix. Every attempt was made to reach a legislative leader or staff person on each of the four caucus committees in all of the states from which data was obtained. Some interviews were impossible, however, when both the legislator and staff refused to talk, and thus there are some gaps in the tables that report the results of inter- views.[32] In total, thirty-one interviews were conducted, thirteen with legislative leaders and eighteen with top staffers, including executive directors of party caucuses, chiefs of staff, or directors of the cam- paign committees. The focus of the interviews was the legislative party caucus committees, though some questions were asked regard- ing the leadership campaign committees.

These interviews provide qualitative support for the inferences derived from analysis of campaign finance data, insure that the con- clusions drawn from the data are not in error, and provide explana- tions for unexpected findings. They are also the sources of the information on the practices of legislative party campaign committees presented in chapter 4.

3
Finances

Legislative party campaign committees included in this analysis vary in the amount of resources they have to use to assist candidates and in how they use those resources. This chapter takes an initial look at the finances of the thirty-eight caucus committees and the twenty-four leadership PACs to provide an indication of the size of these committees and how they differ in size from state to state, and to examine, at the aggregate level, how these committees spend their money.

Legislative Caucus Committees

Aggregate statistics—total funds allocated by the committee to candidates, the percentage of all of the revenues raised by the party's candidates that came from the committees, the mean level of support, and the types of candidates receiving assistance are presented in tables 3-1 through 3-4. Note that these are figures aggregated from candidate receipts and thus will not accurately reflect all of the committees' expenditures. They do not include expenditures for fundraising, overhead, and candidate services that cannot be attributed to individual candidates.

Table 3-1 describes the house party caucus campaign committees and table 3-2 the Senate caucus campaign committees. Large differences in the total funds allocated are obvious, especially when comparing states such as California and New York to Washington and Oregon.[1] In 1986 the Assembly Democrats in California allocated $2,518,068 to candidates for the state assembly, while the House Democratic Caucus in Oregon allocated about one-fiftieth of that, or $40,111, to its party candidates. Similar differences exist among the senate committees, with senate Republicans in New York as the top spenders in 1986 at $1,617,789, and the Indiana Senate Democrats at the bottom, spending $22,650.

Of all funds raised by a party's candidates, the percentage that comes from the caucus committee (also presented in tables 3-1 and 3-2 where possible) demonstrates that the enormous differences between the committees in the sample are not just a matter of the differences in the cost of campaigns in these states.[2] Not only do California and New York legislative party campaign committees out spend their counterparts in the other states in absolute dollars, but they also account for larger proportions of all of the funds raised. In 1986, for example, the New York Republican Caucus Committee's expenditures accounted for 35.5 percent of all of the funds raised by Republican candidates for the assembly, while the funds allocated by the Independent-Republican Caucus Committee in Minnesota constituted only 1.3 percent of the funds raised by Republican candidates. Thus, the level of campaign financing varies greatly among the states included in the sample.

The size of the standard deviations in relation to the means indicates that most of the committees concentrate their resources on a selective number of legislative candidates, with many candidates receiving no assistance. This too varies from state to state, with the committees in California and the Illinois House Republican Campaign Committee, the only committees whose ratio of the standard deviation to the mean reaches 3 to 1, the most efficient at concentrating their resources. The committees in Tennessee, the Illinois Committee to Re-elect a Democratic Senate (until 1986), and the Wisconsin State Senate Democratic Committee and Senate Republican Campaign Committee were the least efficient in concentrating their resources (almost a 1 to 1 ratio). In fact, the Illinois Committee to Re-elect a Democratic Senate funded almost all Democratic candidates to the senate in 1982 and all of the candidates in 1984. All of the rest of the committees tend to have a standard-deviation-to-mean ratio of about 2 to 1, indicating a degree of concentration of resources.

To illustrate what a concentration of resources means for the role of legislative caucus campaign committees, one only need look at some of the most hotly contested seats in these states. For example, in California in 1986 the Assembly Democrats contributed $589,171 to the campaign of Jack Dugan, their candidate for the open seat in the

Table 3-1. House Caucus Campaign Committee Funds for 1982, 1984, and 1986

	1982	1984	1986
California Democrats (Assembly Democrats)			
total funds allocated			$2,518,068
% of Dem. funds raised			22.3%
mean level of support	none	none	33,574
standard deviation			103,347
% incumbents funded			7.5%
% non-incumbents funded			22.9%
California Republicans (Assembly Republican PAC)			
total funds allocated	$363,263	$329,054	$1,256,873
% of Rep. funds raised	5.2%	4.3%	13.5%
mean level of support	4,844	4,635	15,910
standard deviation	11,035	14,994	47,169
% incumbents funded	13.0%	6.5%	3.7%
% non-incumbents funded	42.3%	22.5%	37.3%
Illinois Democrats (Illinois Democratic Majority Committee)			
total funds allocated	$371,728	$391,733	$444,474
mean level of support	3,410	3,497	4,154
standard deviation	6,089	6,261	7,327
% incumbents funded	46.7%	63.0%	62.1%
% nonincumbents funded	37.5%	54.5%	29.3%
Illinois Republicans (House Republican Campaign Committee)			
total funds allocated	$189,544		$551,509
mean level of support	1,954		4,758
standard deviation	3,692	NA	12,899
% incumbents funded	33.3%		17.1%
% nonincumbents funded	32.8%		27.8%
Indiana Democrats (Indiana House Democratic Caucus)			
total funds allocated	$18,400	$37,065	$76,950
mean level of support	195	441	905
standard deviation	238	731	1,667
% incumbents funded	46.2%	46.2%	20.0%
% non-incumbents funded	44.1%	35.6%	34.0%
Indiana Republicans (House Republican Campaign Committee)			
total funds allocated	$52,750	$56,750	$74,500
mean level of support	593	591	847
standard deviation	966	869	1,180
% incumbents funded	79.2%	88.5%	78.6%
% non-incumbents funded	58.3%	34.3%	40.6%
Minnesota Democrats (DFL Caucus Committee)			
total funds allocated	$35,921	$78,050	$45,000
% of Dem. funds raised	2.5%	3.7%	2.2%
mean level of support	268	596	363
standard deviation	240	733	723
% incumbents funded	32.0%	21.2%	15.1%
% non-incumbents funded	95.0%	90.8%	65.1%
Minnesota Republicans (IR Caucus Committee)			
total funds allocated	$29,450	$27,100	$28,300
% of Rep. funds raised	2.1%	1.3%	1.3%
mean level of support	241	210	232
standard deviation	275	249	348
% incumbents funded	40.9%	37.3%	26.7%
% non-incumbents funded	68.4%	53.8%	48.4%
Missouri Democrats (House Democratic Campaign Committee)			
total funds allocated		$28,365	$78,078
% of Dem. funds raised		3.7%	6.3%
mean level of support	did	188	550
standard deviation	not	277	787
% incumbents funded	exist	51.6%	43.3%
% nonincumbents funded		47.5%	40.0%
Missouri Republicans (Missourians Organized for Republican Equality--MORE)			
total funds allocated		$4,400	$12,500
% of Rep. funds raised	did	1.0%	1.8%
mean level of support	not	36	159
standard deviation	exist	186	290
% incumbents funded		14.6%	19.1%
% nonincumbents funded		4.5%	40.7%

Table 3-1—*Continued*

	1982	1984	1986
New York Democrats (Assembly Democrats)			
total funds allocated		$758,868	$944,042
% of Dem. funds raised		18.8%	28.9%
mean level of support	NA	5,539	6,891
standard deviation		11,166	13,746
% incumbents funded		28.6%	29.9%
% non-incumbents funded		47.8%	46.0%
New York Republicans (Assembly Republicans)			
total funds allocated		$377,029	$632,984
% of Rep. funds raised		17.0%	35.5%
mean level of support	NA	2,655	4,620
standard deviation		6,054	9,056
% incumbents funded		16.3%	26.9%
% non-incumbents funded		23.7%	23.5%
Oregon Democrats (House Democratic Caucus)			
total funds allocated	$6,837	$15,734	$40,111
% of Dem. funds raised	1.3%	2.0%	3.7%
mean level of support	120	286	692
standard deviation	291	548	1,560
% incumbents funded	4.3%	4.2%	24.1%
% non-incumbents funded	23.5%	51.6%	51.7%
Oregon Republicans (Project 86)			
total funds allocated	$18,031	$60,825	$102,152
% of Rep. funds raised	3.2%	6.7%	7.9%
mean level of support	306	1,148	1,792
standard deviation	506	2,322	3,326
% incumbents funded	9.5%	0.0%	4.3%
% non-incumbents funded	52.6%	74.3%	58.8%
Tennessee Democrats (House Democratic Caucus)			
total funds allocated	$118,400	$129,385	$129,250
mean level of support	1,600	1,659	1,701
standard deviation	2,096	2,053	1,990
% incumbents funded	53.8%	50.0%	48.1%
% non-incumbents funded	86.4%	78.6%	87.5%
Tennessee Republicans (House Republican Caucus)			
total funds allocated	$86,046	$94,692	$83,919
mean level of support	1,564	1,690	1,399
standard deviation	1,537	1,725	1,502
% incumbents funded	75.0%	82.8%	75.7%
% non-incumbents funded	82.6%	70.4%	56.5%
Washington Democrats (House Democratic Caucus Committee)			
total funds allocated	$47,040	$94,818	$46,207
% of Dem. funds raised	2.7%	4.8%	1.7%
mean level of support	480	977	481
standard deviation	783	1,702	1,018
% incumbents funded	42.9%	12.5%	17.6%
% non-incumbents funded	41.4%	44.8%	33.3%
Washington Republicans (House Republican Caucus Committee)			
total funds allocated	$82,999	$58,262	$39,145
% of Rep. funds raised	4.0%	2.6%	2.0%
mean level of support	883	620	425
standard deviation	1,399	1,409	959
% incumbents funded	40.0%	10.8%	12.1%
% non-incumbents funded	44.4%	36.8%	40.7%
Wisconsin Democrats (Assembly Democratic Committee)			
total funds allocated	$87,330	$74,383	$56,680
% of Dem. funds raised	8.8%	6.3%	5.1%
mean level of support	891	767	683
standard deviation	991	1,126	1,087
% incumbents funded	40.0%	43.5%	23.9%
% non-incumbents funded	65.5%	51.0%	67.6%
Wisconsin Republicans (Assembly Republican Committee)			
total funds allocated	$41,619	$29,427	$41,415
% of Rep. funds raised	4.8%	2.8%	3.7%
mean level of support	478	342	441
standard deviation	573	378	713
% incumbents funded	66.7%	46.9%	32.6%
% non-incumbents funded	75.4%	77.8%	74.5%

Continued on next page

Table 3-1—*Continued*

Sources: State of California Fair Political Practices Commission, General Election: Campaign Receipts and Expenditures and 1982 Legislative Winners. Illinois State Board of Elections, "Annual Report of Campaign Contributions and Expenditures," Legislative Party Committee reports. Indiana State Election Board, "Report of Receipts and Expenditures of a Political Committee." Minnesota Ethical Practices Board, Campaign Finance Summary. Missouri Secretary of State, Campaign Reporting Division, Missouri Annual Campaign Finance Report. Oregon Secretary of State, Elections Division, Summary Report of Campaign Contributions and Expenditures. Tennessee Secretary of State, "Campaign Financial Disclosure Statement: For Contributions and Expenditures of State and Local Political Campaigns in Tennessee." Washington Public Disclosure Commission, Election Financing Fact Book. Wisconsin State Board of Elections, Biennial Report of Wisconsin State Elections Board, vol. 2, Statistical Report.

Table 3-2. Senate Caucus Campaign Committee Funds for 1982, 1984, and 1986

	1982	1984	1986
California Democrats (Senate Democratic Caucus)			
total funds allocated			$91,374
% of Dem. funds raised			1.4%
mean level of support	none	none	4,828
standard deviation			11,201
% incumbents funded			21.4%
% non-incumbents funded			23.8%
California Republicans (Senate Republican PAC)			
total funds allocated	$77,019	$358,500	$819,489
% of Rep. funds raised	2.8%	9.9%	19.5%
mean level of support	4,054	17,926	43,131
standard deviation	11,752	40,612	103,667
% incumbents funded	40.0%	12.5%	0.0%
% non-incumbents funded	14.3%	33.3%	40.0%
Illinois Democrats (Committee to Re-elect a Democratic Senate)			
total funds allocated	$58,852	$73,109	$240,878
mean level of support	1,015	3,481	7,299
standard deviation	977	3,900	11,532
% incumbents funded	91.7%	100.0%	80.0%
% nonincumbents funded	100.0%	100.0%	75.0%
Illinois Republicans (Republican State Senate Campaign Committee)			
total funds allocated	$345,697	$327,000	$806,640
mean level of support	7,202	20,438	22,407
standard deviation	13,752	31,202	48,972
% incumbents funded	25.0%	75.0%	36.4%
% nonincumbents funded	50.0%	75.0%	35.3%
Indiana Democrats (Indiana Senate Democrats)			
total funds allocated	$13,250	$11,410	22,650
mean level of support	552	519	985
standard deviation	737	1,326	2,451
% incumbents funded	62.5%	40.0%	9.1%
% non-incumbents funded	56.3%	12.5%	25.0%
Indiana Republicans (Senate Majority 86)			
total funds allocated	$43,400	$46,150	$70,750
mean level of support	1,887	1,846	3,724
standard deviation	2,276	1,666	3,394
% incumbents funded	90.9%	100.0%	87.5%
% non-incumbents funded	75.0%	71.4%	63.6%
Minnesota Democrats (DFL Senate Caucus Committee)			
total funds allocated	$39,728		$79,108
% of Dem. funds raised	3.0%		3.5%
mean level of support	611		1,217
standard deviation	845	no election	2,156
% incumbents funded	26.5%		27.0%
% non-incumbents funded	93.1%		46.4%
Minnesota Republicans (IR Senate Caucus Committee)			
total funds allocated	$43,700		$83,417
% of Rep. funds raised	3.6%		4.3%
mean level of support	694		1,390

Table 3-2—*Continued*

	1982	1984	1986
(<u>Minnesota Republicans</u>--*continued*)			
standard deviation	758	no election	1,913
% incumbents funded	41.2%		35.0%
% non-incumbents funded	95.5%		52.5%
<u>New York Democrats</u>			
total funds allocated		$346,049	$665,108
% of Dem. funds raised		18.9%	49.2%
mean level of support	NA	6,179	12,549
standard deviation		22,678	37,677
% incumbents funded		12.0%	11.5%
% non-incumbents funded		22.6%	18.5%
<u>New York Republicans</u>			
total funds allocated		$690,337	$1,617,789
% of Rep. funds raised		20.1%	70.8%
mean level of support	NA	12,327	30,524
standard deviation		41.911	79,908
% incumbents funded		30.3%	43.8%
% non-incumbents funded		26.1%	38.1%
<u>Oregon Democrats</u> (Senate Democratic Caucus)			
total funds allocated	$7,515	$4,200	$24,845
% of Dem. funds raised	2.6%	1.5%	5.1%
mean level of support	537	280	1,775
standard deviation	466	579	2,700
% incumbents funded	100.0%	16.7%	50.0%
% non-incumbents funded	40.0%	33.3%	66.7%
<u>Oregon Republicans</u> (Operation 86)			
total funds allocated	$11,900	$35,054	$53,217
% of Rep. funds raised	3.7%	11.2%	9.0%
mean level of support	793	2,921	3,801
standard deviation	1,317	4,385	6,218
% incumbents funded	66.7%	100.0%	25.0%
% non-incumbents funded	66.7%	50.0%	70.0%
<u>Tennessee Democrats</u> (Senate Democratic Caucus)			
total funds allocated	$45,000	$77,000	$55,000
mean level of support	3,500	5,133	3,929
standard deviation	3,246	6,031	3,025
% incumbents funded	83.3%	62.5%	70.0%
% non-incumbents funded	85.7%	57.1%	100.0%
<u>Tennessee Republicans</u> (Senate Republican Caucus)			
total funds allocated	$33,000	$47,500	$72,000
mean level of support	2,750	6,786	6,545
standard deviation	2,768	7,734	4,204
% incumbents funded	37.5%	33.3%	0.0%
% non-incumbents funded	100.0%	75.0%	88.9%
<u>Washington Democrats</u> (Senate Democratic Caucus Committee)			
total funds allocated	$56,207	$79,711	$75,076
% of Dem. funds raised	6.7%	9.6%	2.7%
mean level of support	2,555	3,188	3,128
standard deviation	3,132	2,848	4,591
% incumbents funded	33.3%	75.0%	41.7%
% non-incumbents funded	42.9%	94.1%	91.7%
<u>Washington Republicans</u> (Senate Republican Caucus Committee)			
total funds allocated	$36,808	$52,430	$123,427
% of Rep. funds raised	5.5%	5.2%	4.0%
mean level of support	1,840	2,017	5,610
standard deviation	2,666	3,298	10,206
% incumbents funded	85.7%	50.0%	12.5%
% non-incumbents funded	76.9%	57.1%	42.9%
<u>Wisconsin Democrats</u> (State Senate Democratic Committee)			
total funds allocated	$56,750	$46,640	$48,415
% of Dem. funds raised	14.5%	8.5%	7.8%
mean level of support	3,547	2,744	2,848
standard deviation	2,555	2,680	2,564
% incumbents funded	60.0%	42.9%	50.0%
% non-incumbents funded	42.9%	36.4%	100.0%

Continued on next page

Table 3-2—*Continued*

	1982	1984	1986
Wisconsin Republicans (Senate Republican Campaign Committee)			
total funds allocated	$24,742	$20,096	$49,840
% of Rep. funds raised	6.1%	4.9%	8.9%
mean level of support	1,767	1,435	3,115
standard deviation	1,482	1,426	2,930
% incumbents funded	85.7%	60.0%	85.7%
% non-incumbents funded	85.7%	88.9%	88.9%

Sources: State of California Fair Political Practices Commission, General Election: Campaign Receipts and Expenditures and 1982 Legislative Winners. Illinois State Board of Elections, "Annual Report of Campaign Contributions and Expenditures," Legislative Party Committee reports. Indiana State Election Board, "Report of Receipts and Expenditures of a Political Committee." Minnesota Ethical Practices Board, Campaign Finance Summary. Oregon Secretary of State, Elections Division, Summary Report of Campaign Contributions and Expenditures. Tennessee Secretary of State, "Campaign Financial Disclosure Statement: For Contributions and Expenditures of State and Local Political Campaigns in Tennessee." Washington Public Disclosure Commission, Election Financing Fact Book. Wisconsin State Board of Elections, Biennial Report of Wisconsin State Elections Board, vol. 2, Statistical Report.

fifth district, while the Assembly Republican PAC contributed $146,000 on their candidate Tim Leslie, who won the race with 57.6 percent of the vote. The Illinois Senate race for the thirty-eighth district attracted a total of $157,227 from the two senate caucus campaign committees—$28,840 going to the incumbent, Democrat Patrick Welch, and $128,387 going to the challenger, Republican Thomas Setchell. Welch won with 51.6 percent of the vote.

Also evident in the distribution of resources is the fact that a relatively large percent of nonincumbents received assistance. The data show that not just a few nonincumbents received assistance, but that in most cases, a greater proportion of nonincumbents than incumbents received help. The percent of Republican incumbents running for the Oregon House in 1982 who received support from Project 82 was 9.5 percent, while 52.6 percent of nonincumbent candidates received support. This pattern was maintained in 1984 (when no incumbents received support from Project 84) and in 1986. Indiana Republican House and Senate committees, and the Illinois Democratic Majority Committee are the only three committees that consistently assist more incumbents than nonincumbents, which might be the result of their desire to protect the large number of seats they already hold.

Though records are available for only three years, some interesting trends over time can be seen in the caucus committees' levels of activity. Four trends are apparent. Most of the house and senate caucus committees have grown in terms of resources allocated over the three year period. Project 86 (the Oregon House Republican caucus committee), for example, in 1986 allocated nearly six times the amount it allocated in 1982. In Missouri, neither party had any significant caucus committee activity in 1982, and they both nearly tripled their expenditures from 1984 to 1986. The senate caucus campaign committees demonstrated the most consistent pattern of growth, with all committees increasing their output with the exception of the Tennessee and Wisconsin Democrats. A number of committees demonstrated a level pattern of expenditures, perhaps demonstrating that they have reached a level of stability, or have tapped all of the resources they can from their state.

Some committees fluctuated from year to year, such as the Democratic-Farmer-Labor House Caucus Committee, which distributed more resources in 1984 than it did in 1986 or 1982. The same pattern was evident for the Washington House Democrats and the Tennessee Senate Democrats. This pattern might represent an effort on the part of these committees to reduce the losses that they might have incurred from having a popular president of the opposition party at the top of the ticket. And, finally, two committees' expenditures on candidates declined from 1982 to 1986—the House Republican Caucus Committee in Washington, and the Assembly Democrats in Wisconsin. An examination of the records of the Assembly Democrats in Wisconsin indicates that their overall spending has not decreased, only the expenditures directly attributable to candidates have declined. This finding reflects a change in this particular committee from functioning as a provider of cash and a purchaser of services for candidates to being a more service-oriented organization. The leader of the Wisconsin Assembly Democrats indicated that this indeed was the trend.

Leadership Campaign Committees

Tables 3-3 and 3-4 present the aggregate data on the leadership campaign committees (or leadership PACs). These figures represent the transfers from legislators' campaign committees to other candidates for a seat in their chamber. Just as the legislative caucus committees do, these leadership committees vary greatly in the amount of money they distribute. For example, California Democrats in 1986 transferred 160 times more than their counterparts in Wisconsin ($722,708 compared to $4,451). The low level of activity of Wisconsin legislators in

Table 3-3. Finances of House Leadership Political Action Committees in 1982, 1984, 1986

	1982	1984	1986
California Democrats			
total funds allocated	$2,974,909	$2,475,985	$722,708
% of Dem. funds raised	27.2%	24.2%	6.4%
mean level of support	39,665	32,156	9,636
standard deviation	86,592	98,090	22,044
% incumbents funded	44.1%	32.6%	27.5%
% non-incumbents funded	61.0%	32.3%	40.0%
California Republicans			
total funds allocated	$225,990	$654,751	$200,095
% of Rep. funds raised	3.2%	8.6%	2.2%
mean level of support	3,013	9,222	2,533
standard deviation	6,348	25,510	6,932
% incumbents funded	26.1%	29.0%	1.4%
% non-incumbents funded	40.0%	27.5%	29.4%
Minnesota Democrats			
total funds allocated	$26,032	$65,151	$38,492
% of Dem. funds raised	1.8%	3.1%	1.8%
mean level of support	196	497	310
standard deviation	293	712	612
% incumbents funded	30.6%	57.6%	28.3%
% non-incumbents funded	63.8%	67.7%	49.3%
Minnesota Republicans			
total funds allocated	$9,310	$25,966	$60,775
% of Rep. funds raised	.6%	1.3%	2.8%
mean level of support	77	203	498
standard deviation	157	448	1,230
% incumbents funded	22.7%	39.2%	25.0%
% non-incumbents funded	42.7%	35.1%	35.5%
Missouri Democrats			
total funds allocated		$27,353	$39,933
% of Dem. funds raised		3.6%	3.2%
mean level of support	NA	181	281
standard deviation		376	1,192
% incumbents funded		31.6%	26.8%
% non-incumbents funded		57.5%	62.2%
Missouri Republicans			
total funds allocated		$10,747	$7,318
% of Dem. funds raised		2.3%	1.0%
mean level of support	NA	88	72
standard deviation		651	228
% incumbents funded		19.5%	14.9%
% non-incumbents funded		15.9%	20.5%
Oregon Democrats			
total funds allocated	$4,025	$17,850	$57,275
% of Dem. funds raised	.7%	2.3%	5.3%
mean level of support	71	325	988
standard deviation	161	536	2,017
% incumbents funded	13.0%	25.0%	27.6%
% non-incumbents funded	26.5%	48.4%	41.4%
Oregon Republicans			
total funds allocated	$6,727	$5,912	$18,872
% of Rep. funds raised	1.2%	.7%	1.5%
mean level of support	114	112	331
standard deviation	275	230	793
% incumbents funded	9.5%	0.0%	21.7%
% non-incumbents funded	31.6%	40.0%	32.4%
Washington Democrats			
total funds allocated	$22,070	$40,004	$101,231
% of Dem. funds raised	1.3%	2.0%	3.7%
mean level of support	225	408	1,054
standard deviation	412	845	1,775
% incumbents funded	21.4%	15.0%	25.5%
% non-incumbents funded	32.9%	39.7%	46.7%

Table 3-3—*Continued*

	1982	1984	1986
Washington Republicans			
total funds allocated	$6,150	$11,786	$49,323
% of Rep. funds raised	.3%	.5%	2.5%
mean level of support	65	125	536
standard deviation	287	425	1,231
% incumbents funded	2.5%	8.1%	15.2%
% non-incumbents funded	11.1%	21.1%	39.0%
Wisconsin Democrats			
total funds allocated	$4,527	$1,345	$4,451
% of Dem. funds raised	.5%	.4%	.4%
mean level of support	46	16	54
standard deviation	136	69	164
% incumbents funded	50.0%	15.6%	47.8%
% non-incumbents funded	15.5%	9.3%	13.5%
Wisconsin Republicans			
total funds allocated	$2,678	$4305	$4,000
% of Rep. funds raised	.3%	.1%	.4%
mean level of support	31	44	43
standard deviation	97	107	192
% incumbents funded	23.3%	47.8%	25.6%
% non-incumbents funded	29.8%	23.5%	29.4%

Sources: State of California Fair Political Practices Commission, General Election: Campaign Receipts and Expenditures and 1982 Legislative Winners. Minnesota Ethical Practices Board, Campaign Finance Summary. Missouri Secretary of State, Campaign Reporting Division, Missouri Annual Campaign Finance Report. Oregon Secretary of State, Elections Division, Summary Report of Campaign Contributions and Expenditures. Washington Public Disclosure Commission, Election Financing Fact Book. Wisconsin State Board of Elections, Biennial Report of Wisconsin State Elections Board, vol. 2, Statistical Report.

Table 3-4. Finances of Senate Leadership Political Action Committees in 1982, 1984, 1986

	1982	1984	1986
California Democrats			
total funds allocated	$830,626	$197,595	$2,420,936
% Dem. funds raised	25.0%	5.5%	36.8%
mean level of support	46,146	9,880	127,418
standard deviation	63,422	18,766	228,651
% incumbents funded	62.5%	66.7%	35.7%
% non-incumbents funded	60.0%	27.3%	60.0%
California Republicans			
total funds allocated	$280,720	$129,500	$449,603
% Rep. funds raised	10.2%	3.6%	10.7%
mean level of support	14,775	6,475	23,663
standard deviation	30,403	15,789	52,554
% incumbents funded	60.0%	25.0%	25.0%
% non-incumbents funded	42.9%	25.0%	40.0%
Minnesota Democrats			
total funds allocated	$19,917		$93,962
% Dem. funds raised	1.5%		4.2%
mean level of support	311		1,446
standard deviation	507	no election	2,279
% incumbents funded	39.4%		40.5%
% non-incumbents funded	62.1%		67.9%

Continued on next page

Table 3-4—Continued

	1982	1984	1986
Minnesota Republicans			
total funds allocated	$6,528		$43,150
% Rep. funds raised	.5%		2.2%
mean level of support	107		719
standard deviation	283	no election	1,386
% incumbents funded	17.6%		20.0%
% non-incumbents funded	35.7%		40.0%
Oregon Democrats			
total funds allocated	$2,400	$5,785	$1,700
% Dem. funds raised	.8%	2.0%	.4%
mean level of support	171	386	121
standard deviation	350	726	176
% incumbents funded	0.0%	16.7%	37.5%
% non-incumbents funded	44.4%	44.4%	50.0%
Oregon Republicans			
total funds allocated	$475	$1,350	$5,023
% Rep. funds raised	.1%	.4%	.9%
mean level of support	32	113	359
standard deviation	76	390	612
% incumbents funded	33.3%	0.0%	0.0%
% non-incumbents funded	16.7%	12.5%	70.0%
Washington Democrats			
total funds allocated	$9,528	$6,925	$45,295
% Dem. funds raised	1.1%	.8%	1.3%
mean level of support	433	277	1,887
standard deviation	661	446	3,422
% incumbents funded	11.1%	25.0%	16.7%
% non-incumbents funded	61.5%	41.2%	66.7%
Washington Republicans			
total funds allocated	$1,250	$2,800	$30,550
% Rep. funds raised	.2%	.3%	.3%
mean level of support	63	108	1,389
standard deviation	197	184	3,277
% incumbents funded	0.0%	33.3%	0.0%
% non-incumbents funded	15.4%	28.6%	35.7%
Wisconsin Democrats			
total funds allocated	$1,850	$151	$609
% Dem. funds raised	.5%	.02%	.09%
mean level of support	116	9	36
standard deviation	298	28	74
% incumbents funded	60.0%	0.0%	62.5%
% non-incumbents funded	36.4%	20.0%	0.0%
Wisconsin Republicans			
total funds allocated	$2,930	$298	$515
% Rep. funds raised	.7%	.07%	.09%
mean level of support	209	21	32
standard deviation	336	60	125
% incumbents funded	57.1%	40.0%	0.0%
% non-incumbents funded	42.9%	22.2%	22.2%

Sources: State of California Fair Political Practices Commission, General Election: Campaign Receipts and Expenditures and 1982 Legislative Winners. Minnesota Ethical Practices Board, Campaign Finance Summary. Oregon Secretary of State, Elections Division, Summary Report of Campaign Contributions and Expenditures. Washington Public Disclosure Commission, Election Financing Fact Book. Wisconsin State Board of Elections, Biennial Report of Wisconsin State Elections Board, vol. 2, Statistical Report.

this area is undoubtedly due to the fact that such transfers are considered political action committee transfers, which are strictly regulated by state campaign finance laws.

The proportion of house candidates' funds coming from these transfers, however, does not reach the levels that the caucus committees do, nor is there much difference between states when this figure is examined. The case of California Democrats in 1982 and 1984 is a special one. In those years Speaker Willie Brown's campaign committee acted as the legislative party's central contributor with no significant activity on the part of the caucus committee. Thus, the leadership figures for these years in California are inflated. They are kept in the analysis as leadership funds because they are distinct from caucus committee funds; the Speaker, not the party caucus, exercised complete control over them. The senate leadership PACs follow the same pattern as the house leadership PACs, with the exception of California, where transfers from Democratic state senators accounted for 36.8 percent of all funds raised by Democratic candidates for the senate.

The resources transferred from these committees are concentrated in a few races. By comparing the standard deviation to the mean contribution level this becomes evident. For almost all of the leadership groups, this is a ratio of about two to one. All but six out of the thirty-four sets of party leaders followed the pattern of the caucus committees in funding a greater proportion of nonincumbents than incumbents.

The spending by legislators has risen over the period represented in this study for about half of the groups of legislators. The other half have fluctuated over the period, and two, the Wisconsin Democratic representatives and senators, have reduced this activity to the point of making it insignificant. The decline in Wisconsin, once again, can be attributed to the campaign finance laws classifying such candidate committees as PACs, which severely restricts their activity understate law.

Conclusion

Examination of the aggregate levels of funding of both legislative caucus campaign committees and legislative leadership PACs uncovers some interesting patterns: both concentrate their funds, and most fund a large proportion of nonincumbent candidates. The first pattern is important in light of the fact that many committees, while distributing substantial amounts of money and services, still represent a small proportion of all of the funds raised in legislative elections. If they failed to concentrate their resources, the contribution they could make to any particular race would be, at best, minor and most likely insignificant. The fact that these committees are willing to support nonincumbent candidates, and even support more nonincumbents than incumbents, also has important implications for legislative party campaign committees. By supporting nonincumbents the campaign committees act in ways that are more similar to political parties than to PACs.

Knowing that legislative party campaign committees concentrate their resources and fund nonincumbents is important, but it is more important to know how the resources are concentrated and how much of them are used to assist nonincumbent candidates. This can only be done by analyzing the actual distribution of legislative party campaign resources from the perspective of individual candidates. Such analysis was conducted and is presented in chapters 5, 6, and 7.

4

Legislative Party Campaign Committees: Structures and Practices

That legislative party campaign committees exist in the American states and provide electoral assistance to legislative candidates is about all that is known of these organizations. How they are organized, what types of activities they are involved in, what types of assistance they provide candidates, how they make their decisions, and how they differ from state to state are all mysteries to most political scientists and political observers. The purpose of this chapter is to unravel these mysteries using information obtained in interviews with legislative leaders and caucus staff in the eleven states.

Unraveling these mysteries will make it possible to determine just what these campaign committees are. Are they merely legislative party PACs distributing financial resources? Are they party organizations the purposes of which are to provide party services to candidates, recruit candidates, and pursue party goals? Or are they unique organizations that are neither PACs nor parties? The information culled from the surveys and presented in this chapter suggests that legislative caucus campaign committees are very much like political parties, and not at all like PACs, a conclusion with extremely important implications for our understanding of political party organization at the state level. Leadership campaign committees, on the other hand, more closely resemble PACs, but as the later chapters will demonstrate, the way the allocate their resources makes them unique.

Organization

One of the great things about studying state politics is the rich variety one finds in the way things are done. Legislative caucus campaign committees, with their diversity of organizational forms, are no exception. Some of the caucus campaign committees are composed of all of the members of the caucus, some are actual committees appointed by the party's leaders or elected by the caucus, and some include only the party's leaders. Instead of discussing each caucus campaign committee's organization separately, I will take a comparative approach. One way of looking at caucus campaign committee organization is to arrange the caucus campaign committees on a continuum according to the level of participation afforded caucus members. Figure 4-1 shows where the various caucus campaign committees fall on such a continuum. Each campaign committee is labeled by state, party, and chamber; the first two initials are the state, the last two are the chamber and party.

No interparty differences are evident in the way the committees are organized, but senate committees have a greater tendency to entail more participation from caucus members. Nine out of eleven caucus committees that include all members or that allow the caucus members to select the committee are senate caucus committees. This is not surprising considering the smaller size of the senate chambers.

Figure 4-1 does, however, mask the great number of variations in organization that the interviews uncovered. Three senate committees, the Oregon Republican's and Democrat's, and the Indiana Democrat's are comprised of senators who are not up for reelection. This has interesting implications for how these committees operate because it insulates the committee from the demands of incumbent legislators involved in their own reelection battles.[1] It means that these caucus committees have more freedom to pursue party goals as opposed to individual goals, making it easier for them to support more nonincumbent candidates to build a legislative majority. The level of participation, though, is not necessarily a reflection of power over decision making. To illustrate, the Illinois Democratic Majority Committee in theory includes all legislators, but is in fact run by the speaker who makes the bulk of the decisions in consultation with other Democratic leaders in the house.

Some caucus campaign committees include individuals who are not legislators. The House Republican Campaign Committee in Illinois is comprised of four legislators, the minority leader, and "members of the public," which include corporate heads, interest group representatives, and old "party warhorses," or former party organization members. The House Democratic Campaign Committee in Maine is "a fairly autonomous group" that includes the constitutional

High   Low

All caucus members	All senators not running	Committee selected by caucus	Committee selected by leader	Committee composed of leaders	Leader
IL SD	OR SR	ME SD	IL HR	ME HD	OR HR
WI AR	OR AD	ME SR	CA AD	WA HD	OR HD
TN SR	IN SD		MO HD	IN SR	WI AD
WA SR			MO HR		CA SD
WI SR			NY SR		WI SD
IL HD			NY AD		
			IN HD		
			MN HD		
			WA HR		
			MN SD		
			MN SR		
			WA SD		

S=senate, H=house, A=assembly, D=Democrat, R=Republican
The first two letters indicate the state.

Figure 4-1. Participation of Caucus Members in Campaign Committees

officers elected by the house—the state treasurer and state auditor—in addition to the legislative party leaders—the speaker, minority leader, and whip. The Indiana House Republicans include one county chair on their committee and the party's finance chairman.

A few caucus committees have special subcommittees. The Washington Senate Caucus Committee and the DFL Senate Caucus Committee in Minnesota have separate committees concerned with recruiting candidates for senate contests. And in 1987, the chair of the now defunct California Assembly Democratic Campaign Committee formed a separate committee for voter registration.

Caucus campaign committees also vary greatly in size, ranging from one member to fifteen or greater, and in the involvement of the leaders. Most committees included the leaders, although some, such as the Assembly Democrats in California and the New York Senate Republicans did not include the legislative party's leader.[2] Whether or not the party leaders actually serve on the committee is unrelated to their influence over decisions. In the California case, Speaker Brown exercised enormous control over decisions.

Committee Staff.   All of the caucus campaign committees contacted have staff support for their operation with the exception of the Minnesota and Oregon Senate Republicans. It was frequently and strongly emphasized that, though the staff used for the operation of the caucus campaign committees often came from regular legislative staff, they were hired separately on their own free time. This free time often comes in the form of release time from their regular positions, which is the result of leaves of absence or a reduction to part-time status. Legislative staff did not work on campaigns while on the payroll of the state. Exceptions to the use of part-time staff were found in New York and California. In New York, the Senate Republican Campaign Committee has begun to build and pay for a full-time independent staff—four staff and two consultants in 1988—to handle caucus campaign committee operations. The Assembly Democrats in California had just begun to assemble such a full-time staff before Proposition 73 was passed, effectively banning caucus committees.

Interesting arrangements were found in other states. The Minnesota DFL Caucus Committee hired one staff person to supervise operations and field workers assigned to assist groups of candidates.[3] Indiana House Republicans have part-time staff who were paid for in 1990 by the Republican National Committee. They also have a former chair of the RNC acting as an adviser. In Missouri, the secretaries and staff of the Democratic legislators in the house have formed a separate committee called the House Capitol Democrats Inner-Circle (HCDIC), that staff use to provide services to their bosses campaigns. The type of work they do includes sending out mailings and campaigning door to door on their own time. The HCDIC also meets monthly and even holds fund-raisers.

Leadership and Party Control.   The amount of control that the leadership exercises over the committees' decisions has important implications for the operation of the committees. Figure 4-2 shows where the caucus campaign committees fall in terms of leadership control. The figure was constructed from responses to the question, "how much control would you say the leadership (the speaker, the minority leader, or the majority leader) has over the committee's decisions?" Fifteen out of thirty-one responded that the leadership "makes the decisions." Among this group were the Assembly Democrats in California, a group described as "a board of directors and a CEO, where the CEO [Speaker Willie Brown] controlled 51 percent." Twenty-nine out of thirty-one indicated that either the leaders make the decisions or that they exercise a great deal of control over the committee. Most responses, however, were accompanied by the statement that the leaders take the caucus members' wishes into account by building a consensus or by staying within the boundaries of an implicit understanding of what the resources will be used for. Thus, it appears that most caucus campaign committees are largely run by the party's legislative leaders, with input from the rank-and-file members of the caucus. This is especially clear if one compares figure 4-1 and figure 4-2.

The amount of input or control exercised by the state party organization over legislative party caucus campaign activities has important implications for the strength of political parties in the American states. If the legislative and state parties work together, achieving some level of integration, the party as a whole may function better as a link between officeholders, and consequently strengthen the party organization within the state. Lack of cooperation limits the effect legislative party campaign committees may have on strengthening the party system.

Practically all representatives of the caucus campaign committees indicated that the state party organization exercised no control over their committee's operation (the exception being the Tennessee House Republicans: the respondent indicated that the state party has "some control" over the operations of the caucus committee). The Senate Republican Campaign Committee in New York, for example, operates completely independent of the state central committee despite being, legally, an arm of it.

Though the state central committees were reported to have "no influence" over caucus committee decisions, a great deal of coordination or cooperation exists between the two. Sources in a number of states indicated that their committee cooperated with the state and national parties and that the legislative party committees used state party resources such as mail privileges or phone banks. The Illinois Committee to Re-Elect a Democratic Senate has a unique arrangement because the state chair of the Democratic party is a state senator and serves on the committee. Wisconsin Democrats seem to have reached the highest level of cooperation between the legislative party and the state and national party. In the words of Speaker Thomas Loftus, a "partnership has developed with the state and national organizations" in which the national and state organizations recognize the legislative party as a legitimate party entity.

The situation has recently changed in California, where Proposition 73 has banned the caucus campaign committee practices. Previously the Democratic state party and the Assembly and Senate Democratic Caucus Campaign Committees had little to do with each other. Now, because of ban on caucus committee activity in Proposition 73, the caucus campaign committees have been forced to reassess their relationship with the state party organizations.

No control	Moderate level of control	High level of control	Absolute control
NY SR	MN HD	IL SD	ME SD
		IL HR	OR HR
		ME HD	WI AR
		OR SR	OR SD
		ME SR	CA AD
		IN SD	WA HD
		WA SR	TN SR
		MO HR	IN SR
		MO HD	WI AD
		WA HR	CA SD
		MN SR	WI SR
		WA SD	WI SD
		IN HR	IL HD
			MN SD

S = senate, H = house, A = assembly, D = Democrat, R = Republican
The first two letters indicate the state.

Figure 4-2. Leadership Control in Legislative Party Caucus Committees

Types of Candidate Support Provided

Almost all legislative caucus campaign committees provide both cash and in-kind assistance to candidates. The Tennessee Republican committees and the Maine Senate Republican Committee provide only cash (though the house Republican committee in Tennessee assists candidates with fund-raising and encourages legislators to make personal appearances on behalf of party candidates). Tables 4-1 and 4-2 illustrate the types of services provided by the campaign committees. Services include polling, either from another source or conducted by the committees; campaign consultants; mailing lists; assistance with advertising; campaign seminars; assistance with fund-raising; lists of contributors; assistance with issue papers and positions; research on opposition candidates; demographics research; registration drives; and get-out-the-vote drives.

Some caucus campaign committees provide campaign workers or assistants for the candidates in their districts, a practice usually reserved for the political parties. The Wisconsin House Democrats assign incumbent legislators to specific districts where they can help with advice. According to Betty Jo Nelson, former minority leader, the Wisconsin Republicans have a "buddy system," in which incumbents

Table 4-1. In-kind Assistance Provided by Senate Caucus Campaign Committees

	Polling	Con-sultants	Mailing lists	Adver-tising	Seminars	Fund raising	Lists of con-stituents	Direct mail	Get out votes	Other
Democrats										
California	x	x	x	x	x	x	x			6
Illinois	x	x	x	x	x	x	x	x	x	8
Indiana	x	x	x	x	x	x	x			9
Maine	x		x	x	x	x	x			4
Minnesota	x	x	x	x	x	x	x	x	x	1
Oregon	x			x	x	x				2
Washington	x		x	x	x	x	x			3
Wisconsin		x		x	x	x	x			
Republicans										
Indiana	x		x		x	x	x			5
Maine	cash only				x	x				
Minnesota	x	x	x	x						
New York	x	x	x	x		x	x	x	x	7
Oregon	x	x	x	x	x	x				
Tennessee	cash only					x				
Washington	x	x	x	x	x	x				
Wisconsin	x	x		x	x	x	x			

Note: Table represents the campaign committees before Proposition 73.
1. Offers help with issue papers, a weekly newsletter, staff assistance, access to lobbies, and a photographer to take pictures for campaign literature.
2. Provides issue books for candidates.
3. Helps with press releases, researches opposition candidates, briefs candidates for debates, provides staff, assists with attaining threshold required for public funding and petitions to get on ballot.
4. Conducts fund raiser for candidates.
5. Arranges personal appearances at candidate's fund raisers.
6. Provides demographics research, speech writing, press relations.
7. Coordinates phone banks, maintains computerized voter identification file, registers voters.
8. Coordinates phone banks, maintains precinct lists.
9. Provides brochures, raw film footage of incumbents in action, and nonincumbents in the capital for ads, researches voting records, helps manage campaigns.

Table 4-2. In-kind Assistance Provided by House Caucus Campaign Committees

	Polling	Con-sultants	Mailing lists	Adver-tising	Seminars	Fund raising	Lists of con-stituents	Direct mail	Get out votes	Other
Democrats										
California	x	x	x	x	x	x	x	x	x	7
Illinois	x	x	x	x	x	x	x	x		10
Indiana	x	x	x	x	x	x	x			9
Maine			x	x	x	x	x			4
Minnesota	x		x	x	x	x	x			
Missouri			x	x	x	x	x			
Oregon	x	x	x	x	x	x	x			3
Washington	x	x	x	x	x	x	x			
Wisconsin	x	x	x	x	x	x	x			1
Republicans										
Illinois	x	x	x	x	x	x				
Indiana	x	x	x	x	x	x	x			6
Missouri				x	x	x				8
Oregon	x	x	x	x	x	x	x			
Tennessee						x				5
Washington	x	x	x	x	x	x	x			
Wisconsin	x	x		x		x				2

1. Provides staff.
2. Establishes a "buddy system" for incumbents to assist freshmen legislators in running for reelection.
3. Helps candidates organize their committees, helps with campaign literature, and "exercise[s] a great deal of control in candidates' campaigns."
4. Provides field workers to specific candidates.
5. Arranges personal appearances.
6. Recruits precinct workers, assists with issue development, provides research, sets up speaking appearances by national and state political figures.
7. Coordinates phone banks (local, central, and spanish), acts as liaison to other campaigns, helps with campaign finance reporting.
8. Helps candidates develop campaign plans.
9. Provides layout service for printed material, develops brochures, helps cut radio advertisement, arranges literature drops.
10. Coordinates phone banks, maintains computer voter files.

assist freshmen legislators in learning how to run as incumbents. The Minnesota House and Senate DFL Committees recently revived an old state party practice of hiring field workers to assist groups of candidates and to conduct voter registration and get-out-the-vote drives. The services provided by the Assembly and Senate Democratic Campaign Committees in California before Proposition 73 also included a field organization to conduct get-out-the-vote drives. Since Lee Daniels has become the minority leader in the Illinois House (1984), the HRCC has emphasized the development of a grassroots organization with the goal of recruiting campaign workers in every targeted precinct. The New York Senate Republican Campaign Committee maintains a computerized voter identification file and conducts voter registration and election day activities.

Because of the emphasis on services, most committees distribute their resources over the whole general election cycle. All but one respondent indicated that their committee makes adjustments in terms of which candidates receive support over the course of the election. Polling, subjective assessments of the candidate's effort, the resources the opposition is putting into the race, and the viability and need of the candidate are the types of information used to make the adjustments.

Much of what the committees provide is candidate-specific; that is, it benefits the candidate only. Activities such as helping candidates cut television or radio commercials, providing them with campaign consultants and poll results, and assisting them with fund-raising, unlike voter mobilization activities, benefit only individual candidates and fail to strengthen the party as a whole. The provision of these services is a reflection of the change in the role played by political parties in the 1980s. Party organizations, especially those at the national level, have adapted to the cash economy of candidate-centered campaigns by becoming "broker" organizations, providing services that for all but the wealthiest candidates are too expensive for them to obtain on their own.[4]

Finally, some committees provided unique services. The Oregon Senate Democrats, for example, hire a photographer to take pictures of legislators for campaign literature. The senate Democrats in Maine follow a similar practice. They provide raw film footage to incumbents, featuring them in action, and to nonincumbents, featuring them in the capital with prominent leaders. This film footage can then be used in the candidate's television advertisements. The California Assembly Democrats had a large phone bank system set up, including centralized and local phone banks, and a spanish language phone bank. And the Wisconsin Senate Democratic Caucus helps candidates reach the threshold necessary to obtain public funds.

It is important to note that, because party organizations obtain services at a discount and provide them at a discount to candidates, the financial data reported by the committees may underestimate the real level of support. In other words, the significance of legislative party campaign committee activity may be even greater than their financial records indicate. This was illustrated by Speaker Miller of New York who stated that "We [the Assembly Democrats] can do things a lot cheaper. We can mail cheaper because of the permit. . . . We have our own printing press, so we can print cheaper. And we can buy in bulk services which you can't do locally. So if you buy a pollster to do fifteen polls, it is cheaper than fifteen candidates each going and hiring their own."[5] In addition, the committees also may not accurately assess the monetary value of a service when filling out a campaign expenditure report because of the difficulty of assigning a monetary value to such things. The undervaluation of services also occurs with the congressional committees. One such practice is to hold onto poll data until its monetary value is significantly decreased (according to FEC laws). The congressional committees then give the poll to a candidate's organization which reports the in-kind contribution at its reduced cost.[6]

That the committees provide so many services in addition to cash contributions is significant for the caucus campaign committees. It means that the legislative parties are functioning not merely as loose organizations distributing cash, but as service organizations closely resembling party organizations. This point is especially clear when the campaign committees provide campaign workers to candidates and get involved in voter mobilization activities, namely, voter registration drives and get-out-the-vote campaigns. Furthermore, five respondents volunteered the fact that their campaign committee places an emphasis on services over cash contributions. By emphasizing in-kind contributions, the caucus campaign committees will not only have a great deal of control over the use of their resources, but they will also have a great deal of influence over what type of campaigns the supported candidates run. If, for example, the committee provides mostly media assistance, the candidate would be forced to lead a media-oriented campaign.

Instead of providing cash to a candidates who have made unwise use of contributions in the past, the Indiana Senate Democrats buy what the candidates need for their campaign. To illustrate the type of expenditures they considered unwise, Indiana Senate Minority Leader Dennis Neary told of one candidate who used the caucus campaign committee's money to purchase a cow at a county fair.

Fund-Raising. In addition to providing contributions of cash and services, caucus campaign committees have an effect on other sources of revenue for candidates. Sixteen of the campaign committees actually direct PAC, individual, and corporate contributions either by actively soliciting these contributions for candidates or by referring friendly contributors to candidates. The Indiana House Democratic Caucus "sits down with interest groups to discuss which races to target," resulting in a situation in which, according to William Schreiber (the Democratic Speaker's executive assistant), "for every one dollar we [the caucus committee] raise, we direct two dollars of interest group money." Charles Pray, president of the Maine Senate, indicated that the senate Democratic caucus campaign committee provides a "matchmaking service" for PACs and candidates by "identifying a candidate's philosophy with PACs and connecting them." The majority leader of the New York Senate holds cocktail parties and invites friendly Republican contributors so they can be introduced to candidates. Since Proposition 73 has been passed in California, this matchmaking function of the party caucus is the only thing caucus members are still legally allowed to do to assist fellow candidates for the legislature.

Of the fifteen committees that do not direct other contributors, seven indicated that the assistance their caucus campaign committee gives to candidates helps candidates raise money from other sources. Contributors see assistance from the caucus campaign committees as a mark of candidate legitimacy. Kathleen Hamilton, staff director for the Senate Democratic Caucus in California, said, "the first thing that PACs ask candidates is, 'Is the SDCC supporting you, and how much?' " Rick Heffley, the executive director of the HRCC in Illinois said that "if you're not targeted by the HRCC, most givers will not be willing to contribute." And a source in the Oregon House Democratic caucus said, "if the leadership says they [candidates] are on the list of 'friends,' PACs and other contributors know it is a good investment and will contribute." Conversely, caucus committees in Wisconsin do not help candidates raise PAC money because of the role of public funding in legislative campaigns.

Because caucus campaign committees direct or influence the giving patterns of other contributors, their influence in legislative politics goes well beyond what they spend on their candidates. This was clearly illustrated in an interview with Jeff Estich, Indiana's speaker pro tempore. He said the House Republican Campaign Committee was stronger than the Indiana House Democratic Caucus, but that the Democrats' alliance with the Indiana State Teachers Association made their caucus campaign committee more effective.

Some of the caucus campaign committees also have a hand in directing leadership campaign committee funds (i.e., the transfer of legislators' personal campaign funds to other candidates). The House Democrats in Oregon and Washington have an arrangement under which the legislative caucus campaign committee actually directs the transfer of funds from legislators' committees. This similarity between adjacent states is no accident. It is reportedly the result of a friendship between the Washington Speaker and the Oregon Majority Leader. The Oregon House Republicans also coordinate the transfer of candidates' funds.

Recruiting.   Not only do the legislative caucus campaign committees provide services, but they are also actively involved in recruiting candidates—another traditional party organization role. All of the committees contacted, with the exception of the Tennessee House Republicans and Maine Senate Republicans, were involved in recruiting candidates. In fact, six of the respondents indicated that the recruitment role was a "very important" function of the legislative caucus campaign committee. All of these six respondents were legislators or staff involved in senate caucus campaign committee operations. According to Gail Gonzales, executive director of the State Senate Democratic Committee in Wisconsin, recruiting is a "big responsibility [of the SSDC, which] feels it is their role to have a Democratic candidate in every district." The California Assembly Democratic Committee also wanted a Democrat running in every assembly district. They accomplished this in the 1988 election. The importance of recruiting is reflected in the fact that the Minnesota Senate Democrats and the Washington Senate Republicans actually have subcommittees of their caucus campaign committees for the purpose of recruiting candidates.

Twenty-four of the caucus campaign committees also use the assistance available from the caucus to induce candidates to run, three committees "discuss the availability" of help from the caucus campaign committee, and one said that the committee uses the availability of help to "encourage" candidates to run; the respondent thought "induced" was too strong a word. This practice is not universally applied to all candidates, however. "We only use the availability of resources from the DFL Caucus Committee as an inducement in districts where there is a good chance of winning. . . . We are honest with the candidates," said Ann Wynia, the majority leader of the Minnesota House. Anne Kalich, the Speaker's executive assistant in Washington stated that, "they [the candidates] have to show us more than we show them. . . . They have to prove they can raise money first. It is an incentive program. Assistance comes when they prove they are viable candidates."

The fact that legislative party caucus campaign committees recruit candidates adds another piece of evidence in support of the importance of these committees. In affecting the pool of candidates, the committees affect the competitiveness of races and ultimately improve the choices available to the voter in legislative elections. In performing this role, the legislative party, and the party in general, increases its influence in an area of party politics that they had lost to primary elections: selecting party candidates. This influence could be even greater if the legislative caucus campaign committees backed their recruited candidates in contested primary elections.

Sources in fifteen of the committees indicated that their caucus campaign committee supported candidates before primary contests. But for six of those committees, providing support during primary elections was mainly to get an early start on the general election campaign. This happens often in states in which the general election season is shortened by a late primary, namely Washington, Wisconsin, and Minnesota. According to Anne Kalich, the Washington Speaker's executive assistant, "it [providing assistance in primaries] is done to get a jump on the general election. If two candidates are running in a primary, neither will get any assistance." The House Republicans in Washington will assist both candidates equally in a contested primary so that the best candidate will win. In New York, the parties, including the caucus campaign committees, are banned by state law from supporting candidates in contested primaries.

Some respondents, however, indicated that caucus campaign committee assistance was provided for candidates in contested primaries. This happened mainly in the case of an incumbent facing a challenger, or sometimes when the campaign committee recruited a candidate. The Indiana Senate Democrats "work behind the scenes" to help a recruited candidate. In Minnesota, where the parties have a preprimary endorsing system, the DFL House Caucus supports endorsed candidates in contested primaries. The DFL House Caucus has also supported incumbents that were not endorsed by the party convention against their endorsed opponents. One of the caucus campaign committees in Oregon supports incumbent candidates with primary opponents. The Washington Senate Republicans provide assistance in primary races for both purposes—getting an early jump on the general election and winning a contested primary. The Wisconsin Assembly Democrats have supported candidates in contested primaries but no longer do so because of past failures. And in California, the tradition of carrying leadership battles over to primary contests continued up to 1988.[7] In the primary of that year, the Assembly Democratic Campaign Committee fended off a challenge from the "gang of five," a group of Democrats opposed to Brown's speakership, in a primary battle over assembly district 63.

In summary, legislative party caucus campaign committees provide a wide variety of services, some traditional party services, others more in line with today's candidate-centered campaigns. Caucus campaign committees provide cash contributions. They have an effect on contributions candidates receive from other sources. They actively recruit candidates and sometimes get involved in primary battles. Thus, these legislative caucus campaign committees are candidate service organizations that appear to be very similar to the typical political party organization. Such a finding has major implications for political parties and legislative elections. For instance, it means that Sorauf's distinction between the party-in-government and the party organization is becoming less rigid because the legislative parties-in-government are now involved in campaigning in addition to governing.[8]

Caucus Campaign Committee Revenues

The services provided by the caucus campaign committees have important implications for legislative elections and the way that legislative parties are perceived. Where these committees get their funds has implications for legislative behavior and public policy. Help from caucus campaign committees might provide candidates with insulation from special interests by removing or lessening the debt candidates owe as a result of accepting campaign contributions. On the other hand, caucus campaign committees might also provide an easier, more centralized way for interest groups to have an influence if the caucus is in debt to a contributing group. I asked respondents from where the caucus campaign committees received their money.[9] Tables 4-3 and 4-4 present the sources of funding for the caucus

Table 4-3. Sources of Funds for Senate Caucus Campaign Committees

	Individuals	Business PACs	Labor PACs	Profes-sional PACs	Legis-lators	State Party	National Party	Local Party	Other
Democrats									
California	x	x	x	x	x				
Illinois	x	x	x	x	x	x	x	x	
Indiana	x	x	x	x	x	x			
Maine	x	x	x	x	x				
Minnesota	x		x	x	x			x	1
New York	x	x	x	x					
Oregon	x	x	x	x			x		
Tennessee	x	x	x	x	x			x	1
Washington	x	x	x	x	x				1
Wisconsin	x	x		x					2
Republicans									
California	x	x		x	x	x	x	x	1
Illinois	x	x		x	x		x		1
Indiana	x	x		x	x				
Maine	x	x		x	x				
Minnesota	x	x	x	x	x	x	x		
New York	x	x	x	x	x	x	x	x	1
Oregon	x	x	x	x				x	1
Tennessee	x	x	x	x	x				
Washington	x	x		x		x	x		
Wisconsin	x	x		x		x	x	x	1

1. Corporations
2. Fund raisers

Table 4-4. Sources of Funds for House Caucus Campaign Committees

	Individuals	Business PACs	Labor PACs	Professional PACs	Legislators	State Party	National Party	Local Party	Other
Democrats									
California	x	x	x	x	x				1
Illinois	x	x	x	x	x	x	x	x	
Indiana	x	x	x	x	x	x	x	x	1
Maine	x	x	x	x	x				
Minnesota	x	x	x	x	x				
Missouri	x	x	x	x	x				1
New York	x	x	x	x	x				1
Oregon	x	x	x	x	x	x	x		
Tennessee	x	x	x	x	x			x	1
Washington	x	x	x	x					
Wisconsin	x	x	x	x					
Republicans									
California	x	x	x	x	x	x	x		1
Indiana	x	x		x		x	x		2
Illinois	x	x	x	x	x	x	x	x	1
Missouri	x	x		x	x				1
New York	x	x	x	x	x		x		1
Oregon	x	x	x	x	x				1
Tennessee	x	x		x	x				1
Washington	x	x	x	x	x				
Wisconsin	x	x		x	x			x	

1. Corporations
2. Congressmen and statewide candidates

committees. The information was drawn from interviews and from the financial records of the committees.

Caucus campaign committees receive contributions from individuals, PACs, caucus members, the state party organization, the national party organization, local parties, and corporations. Every campaign committee received some contributions from individuals and some from political action committees. The type of PACs that contributed to the caucus committee varied slightly according to the party, with more Republican committees receiving business PAC money and more Democratic committees receiving labor PAC money. Labor PACs, for example, contributed to all twenty-one of the Democratic caucus campaign committees while only contributing to nine Republican committees.

Legislators were another source of funds for a large number of the caucus campaign committees. Most committees contacted received contributions from their own caucus members. This means that individual legislators have input into the committees that they contribute to: if they do not like what the committee is doing, they can stop supporting it. It also increases the insulation between beneficiaries of caucus campaign committee support and special interests by putting an extra step between the interest group contribution and the candidate who receives caucus committee support. Finally, if the campaign committees give to close races, the contributions will have an interesting redistributional effect. Most campaign contributors—PACs and individuals—will give money to candidates who are most likely to win (incumbents). This results in a system in which the rich candidates get richer and the poor candidates cannot attract the resources necessary to win. With "wealthy" legislators donating their money to the caucus committees, which in turn distribute it to needy candidates—i.e., those in close races—the effects of the system are reversed. The result is an ultimate distribution of campaign resources that concentrates the resources in closely contested districts. By increasing the competitiveness of a number of marginal seats, this redistribution of resources by legislative party campaign committees has some interesting normative implications for the democratic nature of legislative elections. Specifically, the caucus committees may be responsible for enhancing competition for legislative seats.

Only eleven of the caucus campaign committees receive contributions from state party organizations, while sixteen receive contributions from the national committees. Apparently, the wealth of the national parties is having an impact on the legislative parties. Sources indicate that the contributions from the Democratic National Committee and the Republican National Committee will increase as time for reapportionment draws near. The involvement of the national and state parties in legislative elections through the caucus committees and on their own raises some interesting questions, namely: How do the national, state, and legislative parties differ in targeting races? Do they work together, or do they cooperate to cover as many races as possible? One indication comes from Wisconsin. Speaker Loftus said that the Assembly Democrats cooperate closely with the state and national parties. The former head of the Wisconsin Assembly Republicans, Betty Jo Nelson, indicated that the Republican caucus campaign committee coordinates activities with the state party to "avoid duplication." The House Republican Campaign Committee in Illinois receives some contributions from congressional candidates and candidates for statewide offices.

Some caucus campaign committees, such as the Indiana House Republicans, the Washington Senate Republicans, and the Wisconsin Senate Republicans, raise money through direct mail campaigns. A particularly interesting case in fund-raising is the Washington Senate Republicans. They have established a major donor program in which individuals can purchase membership for five hundred dollars a year or one thousand dollars per corporation. The benefits of membership include invitations to meetings with the Republican Senators every two to three months to discuss issues. The Tennessee Senate Republicans raise all of their funds from an annual fund-raiser that is held while the legislature is not in session. Thus, legislative party caucus campaign committees have cultivated a variety of sources to fund their campaign activities. Each committee depends on no less than four different sources for their funds. This diversity of supporters makes the committees broad-based organizations, not organizations representing narrow interests, and they are, in this way, similar to political party organizations. The fact that the caucus committees receive contributions from a variety of sources might mean that there is little danger of interest groups gaining centralized influence over policy through the caucus committees. Such an assertion, however, assumes that the universe of contributors provides adequate representation of all interests in society on the issues that come before the legislature, and that is a dubious assumption.

Trends

State legislative party campaign committees have been around since the late 1970s, though many of them did not become very active until the 1980s. Among the older caucus campaign committees are those in Illinois, New York, Minnesota, Washington, Wisconsin, and California. The younger committees are those in Tennessee, Indiana, Maine, Missouri, and Oregon. During the interviews legislators and staff were asked whether or not they were cognizant of any changes that have occurred in the operation of their caucus committee. Most respondents indicated that their committee had undergone some change in the past ten to fifteen years. Not surprisingly, the changes most often mentioned were in the size and sophistication of the operation and in the types of assistance provided candidates.

It appears that most of the legislative caucus campaign committees started out as organizations that simply distributed, or redistributed, money. When asked if they were aware of any changes in their caucus committee, eleven legislators or staff members volunteered that a change had occurred in the form of the assistance they provided candidates and that they had moved from providing cash toward providing services. The Committee to Re-Elect a Democratic Senate in Illinois, for example, has "moved from providing mostly money to providing a whole array of services," according to Bill Holland, Senate President Rock's chief of staff. According to Speaker Thomas Loftus of Wisconsin, the Assembly Democratic Committee began as a money distributing organization, evolved into a campaign headquarters, and now, with the variety of activities they perform, has developed into a party organization. More recently, a change is occurring in the Indiana Senate Republican's committee, according to President Pro Tempore Robert Garton, who indicated that the committee is just beginning to expand its services for the 1990 elections. The fact that all of the older caucus campaign committee organizations have evolved into service providers, and the fact that the committees that provide little or no services are the more recently developed committees, provide strong indications that as the campaign committees mature they tend to evolve into more service-oriented party organizations.

A few legislators or staff members indicated that a change had occurred in the emphasis in the types of candidates supported, from incumbents to nonincumbents. One staff person employed by the Washington House Democratic Caucus campaign committee indicated that in the past the committee had given across the board contributions to all incumbents. Now they concentrate their resources on close races. This was also the case for the Illinois House Democratic Majority Committee. Sources from the Democrats in Oregon's House,

Republicans in Tennessee's House, and Democrats in Indiana's Senate mentioned that their campaign committees have moved away from a strong or sole emphasis on incumbent candidates. All but one of the caucus committees will fund nonincumbent candidates. Some of the younger caucus committees, though, are still very much "incumbent protection associations." Charles Webster, the Republican minority leader of the Maine Senate indicated that the senate Republican's committee was "originally formed to help incumbents get reelected . . . and that that has remained its purpose." The house campaign committees in Missouri, which came into existence after 1984, are more like incumbent trust funds than caucus committees at this time. Incumbents are the main contributors to the campaign committees, and as an election draws near their money is returned to them if they need it. The house Democratic Campaign Committee also gives bonuses back to candidates who contributed. The house Republican committee (M.O.R.E.) uses the left over funds for other committee purposes, one of them to fund other candidates.

The changes indicated in the interviews suggest that the caucus campaign committees have evolved, or are still in the process of evolving. Some of the committees have developed quite far, becoming complex service organizations resembling political party organizations. These include the Wisconsin, New York, California, Illinois, and Minnesota caucus committees (all among the oldest committees). Other committees are still at the early stages of development. Indiana committees are only beginning to become service oriented. Legislative party caucus campaign committees in Tennessee, Maine (Republicans only), and Missouri are at the earliest stage; their operations consist of the party caucuses mainly raising and distributing cash contributions.

If all of the caucus committees in all of the states listed in chapter 1 continue to evolve in this manner, the party organizational structure at the state level may quickly come to resemble the structure of the national party organizations, with active legislative party organizations separate from the central committees. For the New York Senate Republicans this is a legal reality, and the fact that they are building a full-time independent staff is an indication that it is becoming an organizational reality as well.

One state to watch is California. Proposition 73, passed by voters in 1988, outlawed the current form of the caucus campaign committees and placed a five thousand dollar limit on party contributions to candidates. Caucus campaign committees cannot operate under the terms of the proposition because it prohibits a candidate from controlling more than one committee. Thus, no California legislator can run a caucus campaign committee in addition to his own campaign committee, as had been done previously. Transfers of funds between candidate committees were also banned.

According to Michael Galizio, Speaker Brown's chief of staff, Proposition 73 puts the Democrats in California at a particular disadvantage because they relied heavily on the caucus campaign committees and candidate transfers to support legislative candidates. Republicans had relied on the state party organization and "Lincoln Clubs"—Republican clubs that raise large sums of money from individuals by bundling the money for candidates—and therefore will not suffer under the proposition. In fact, the parties vigorously campaigned on opposite sides of the proposition.

The legislative parties are in the process of adjusting to the new law. Galizio reported that the caucus members are now limited to making appearances at fund-raisers for other candidates and directing "good campaign people" to campaigns that need them. They cannot, however, pay their salaries. The caucus is also looking into increasing the participation of the state party organization and the use of independent committees. Kathleen Hamilton, director of the Senate Democratic Caucus, indicated that the caucuses were looking into two possible options. One option being considered, is cooperation for the first time with the state party organization and having the party take over some of the functions that were previously the responsibility of the caucus campaign committee. The other option is to set up a nonprofit organization to provide electoral services for candidates. The latter option sounds suspiciously like a political party—an inference that was not lost on Hamilton.

Perceptions of the Impact of the Committees

An attempt was made during the interviews to get the legislator's or the staff person's perceptions regarding the effect of caucus campaign committee activity. This involved asking questions about the perceived effectiveness of the caucus campaign committee activity and the impact they felt the committee's activity had on legislative behavior and elections.

All respondents indicated that the purpose of the caucus committee was to gain or maintain a majority of seats. When asked how effective the committee was at achieving that goal about half stated emphatically that it was very effective, while the rest believed that the committee was somewhat effective or not very effective. No respondent indicated that they thought the caucus committee was ineffective at achieving the goal of majority party status. Charles Webster, minority leader of the Maine Senate, however, did state that the senate Republican's caucus committee was "not a major factor in Maine politics."

Twenty-seven respondents indicated that they believed that their caucus campaign committee had "some impact" or a "significant impact" on the outcome of legislative elections. Senator Houck of Oregon, the minority leader, went so far as to say that the Republican caucus campaign committee played a "critical" role in legislative elections. Bob Haggerty, the executive director of the New York Senate Republican Campaign Committee stated that "in the campaign cycle we believe that we provide that edge of support a candidate needs, making up for some of the weaknesses of the state party." And in Illinois, according to Rich Heffley, the executive director of the House Republican Campaign Committee, the HRCC has a "major impact [on elections] because some seats are up to around one hundred thousand dollars [in campaign costs] and the districts do not have the ability to raise that kind of money." Only four respondents believed that the committee played a minor role in elections, including the Tennessee Senate Republicans and the Maine senate Republicans.

As for the effect legislative party caucus campaign committee activity has on legislative behavior, ten respondents indicated that they believed that it increased party cohesiveness. It appears that this increased cohesion comes more from working together than from any ideological screening of candidates based on voting records or general philosophy. Betty Jo Nelson, the Wisconsin Assembly Minority Leader, stated that the caucus campaign committee has made candidates "feel that they have a friend in the legislature . . . a change from past years." Thomas Loftus, the Wisconsin Speaker, indicated that the participatory nature of the campaign activities of the Democratic caucus campaign committee have created a collegial atmosphere, increasing party cohesion. Furthermore, a couple of legislators and staff made it very clear that political philosophy was not a factor in deciding which candidates to support. Senator Pray of Maine, for example, asserted that the committee does not pay any attention to voting record, he believes that the committee does however, help bring the caucus together. And though Bill Holland of the Committee to Re-

Elect a Democratic Senate feels that the committee has increased cohesion to a certain degree, he noted that "Senator Rock focuses on electing Democrats, [and] not particular types of Democrats." Seven respondents indicated that the caucus campaign committees activities made it easier for the leaders to run the legislature.

One example of the committees having an effect on the relationship between the parties was found in Illinois. Rich Heffley of the HRCC observed that "the 1988 election was very bitter, and it increased the partisanship in the legislature," so much so that for the first time in recent years partisanship "overrode regional divisions [city, suburban, and downstate] within the legislature."

Five respondents indicated that the campaign activity of caucuses causes some divisiveness among caucus members. Dennis Neary, Democratic minority leader in the Indiana Senate, said that some of the safe incumbents became angry when they did not receive any of the benefits of the caucus campaign committee. "Some incumbents are unhappy; they don't see the advantage of majority status, though they are only one less than half, [they] have been in the minority too long." In California, legislative campaign committees (leadership PACs and caucus committees) became significant actors in state legislative elections as part of internal party battles for speaker.

Ten respondents indicated that they believed that the caucus committee activity had no effect on the behavior of legislators within the legislature. This viewpoint was stated best by Ann Wynia, the majority leader of the Minnesota House, who said, "Coming from one who just finished a session trying to twist arms, it has no impact. . . . Candidates assume they will get help no matter what they do."

The responses to the surveys on these perceptual items provide an initial glimpse at the effects that legislative party caucus committees have on legislative politics. Asking about the effect of the caucus committees is obviously not the most rigorous way to determine if the committees do have an impact on elections and legislative behavior. Legislators and staff are not likely to openly answer all questions, some of which may be perceived as sensitive. The fact that some legislators and staff willingly stated that the campaign committee's activity did have a significant impact on legislative elections and on legislative behavior is thus significant. It adds to the evidence indicating the importance of the development of caucus committees, and it also means that this may be a worthwhile area for future research.

Leadership Campaign Committee Funds

Finally, a few questions were asked regarding leadership campaign committees. The first thing to note is that the practice of transferring personal campaign funds to another candidate occurs in all of the states in the sample.[10] All but two of the interviewees indicated that the transfer of leadership campaign committee funds was done with some coordination with the legislative caucus campaign committee. Thus, the leadership PACs in many cases augment the work of the caucus campaign committees. For example, in Missouri, the House Democratic Campaign Committee maintains a list of candidates to target that it supplies to legislators who want to contribute to other campaigns. This practice "adds twenty-five thousand dollars to the HDCC's influence," according to Mark Ausmus, the Speaker's general counsel.

One reason often given for the transfer of funds from leaders' campaign committees to other candidates was to gain or maintain party control of the legislature. Washington Senate Republican Majority Leader, Jeannette Hayner, emphatically stated this position: "It has nothing to do with promoting our [legislators'] own careers. It has everything to do with electing more Republicans!" Though it would make sense that these legislators would use their funds to further their career in the legislature, several legislators went out of their way to deny that this was the purpose, including Jeannette Hayner (above) and James Talent, the Missouri minority leader, who stated that leadership campaign committees are "not used to affect leadership races." Instead, it was "a question of me trying to help others who need it."

The situation is different in New York and California where the transference of funds has been used to promote individual legislators' candidacies for leadership positions. In California it had become part of the Speaker's duties to raise and distribute money.[11] And in New York, leadership candidates contribute funds to candidates who support them, according to Bob Haggerty, the executive director of the Senate Republican Campaign Committee.

Legislators also have much more discretion in what they do with their funds. This is illustrated by comments made about leadership PACs in Maine. Ken Allen, the executive assistant to the speaker, said that the speaker "sticks with the same kind of priorities as the HDCC but is more willing to take a risk and make on-the-spot decisions." Charles Webster, Republican senate minority leader, indicated that he uses his own funds to help candidates in primary contests in order to help win a majority.

The legislators tended to distribute their funds based upon need, i.e., the closeness of the race. This finding should lead to the expectation that there would be no difference between caucus campaign committees and leadership PACs. As the following chapters demonstrate, this is not the case.

One interesting development was mentioned by Representative Wynia, DFL majority leader in Minnesota. A number of women, including herself, have formed a DFL women's caucus which provides campaign money to women candidates. Recently the Independent-Republican (IR) women formed a similar committee of their own. Such a development provides some indication that caucus committees may be effective at more than just promoting members of a political party.

Conclusion

Several conclusions about legislative party campaign committees should be evident from this chapter. First, legislative party campaign committees in the American states display a rich variety of forms and practices. Second, most of the legislative caucus campaign committees have become very much like political party organizations and have an impact that goes well beyond what their financial records indicate. Some committees have already attained a status of institutionalization that approximates the status of party organizations. Other committees are still in the process of evolving into party-like organizations. The perceptions of those who were interviewed regarding the effect of these committees on legislative elections and legislative behavior indicate that it is likely that they are playing an important role in both of these areas. As they continue to grow, legislative party caucus committees' effect can only grow greater.

The finding that the committees vary in the level of institutionalization demands some explanation. It may be due to a number of different factors. The fact that the oldest committees are the most developed indicates that time plays an important role. Factors such as strong party leadership, party competition, and the practices of the other party caucuses, or party caucuses in neighboring states may also effect the speed of development.

In addition to providing some basic information about the committees, this chapter has shown that the development of the legislative party campaign committees is extremely significant. This development has the potential to change the shape of legislative politics and the nature of party organizations at the state level. How effectively these committees distribute the resources they have amassed is crucial to determining the importance of the development of legislative party campaign committees. The distribution of legislative campaign committee resources and the differences between the committees in their campaign behavior is the subject of the empirical analysis that constitutes the remainder of this book.

5

The Allocation
of Resources:
Competitiveness
and Incumbency

We have determined how legislative party campaign committees operate, the activities they are involved in, and the type of assistance they provide to candidates. The next task is to examine how they distribute their resources. In the next three chapters the question of resource distribution will be analyzed using campaign finance data from the ten states. This chapter tests the propositions that the campaign committees concentrate their resources in competitive races and are willing to fund caucus outsiders, in other words, nonincumbent candidates.

A major underlying theme of this research is that the extent of the impact that legislative party campaign committees have on legislative politics is dependent upon the way these campaign committees operate. It was demonstrated in the previous chapter that legislative party caucus campaign committees follow practices that maximize the role of these committees in legislative elections. What remains to be seen, however, is how the legislative party campaign committees actually allocate their resources, which is an integral part of determining the effect these committees have. If legislative party campaign committees concentrate their resources on competitive races, and if these committees are willing to fund nonincumbent candidates, they will play an important role in legislative elections. The propositions developed within the theoretical framework of chapter 2 suggest that, contrary to conventional wisdom regarding the distribution of resources valuable to reelection, we should expect to find that legislative party campaign committees do just that.

The purpose of the analysis presented in this chapter is to test the relationship between the level of assistance received by candidates, the nature of the race they are in, and their incumbency status. More specifically, this chapter provides an empirical test of the first three hypotheses developed in chapter 2. The hypotheses to be tested are:

1. Legislative party campaign committees should be found to concentrate their resources in close races.
2. Legislative party campaign committees should be just as likely to fund nonincumbent candidates in competitive races as incumbent candidates, all other factors being equal.
3. Campaign committees existing in states with low levels of interparty competition will not meet the expectations of hypothesis 2; in other words, they will not necessarily be more likely to fund nonincumbents.

Tests of these hypotheses involve an analysis of contributions, cash and in-kind, received by state house and senate candidates from legislative caucus campaign committees and leadership PACs. Data derived from the interviews with legislative leaders provide supplemental evidence to corroborate and explain the statistical analysis of the campaign finance data.

Close Races, Candidate Status, and Resource Distribution

To determine how legislative party campaign committees allocate their resources, the contributions received by state senate and house candidates were analyzed and compared to the expectations spelled out in the hypotheses. Analysis of campaign committee contributions to house candidates was done using ordinary least squares regression. One set of analyses was conducted for each party committee in each state, regressing the level of assistance provided each candidate on a measure of the closeness of the race and incumbency status. Because most state senate elections included too few cases to obtain meaningful regression results, the campaign committees' contributions to senate candidates were examined using categorical analysis. Analysis of state party contributions, from states where such figures were available, was included for the sake of comparison.

The margin of defeat or victory for the party's candidate in the previous election was used as an indicator of the closeness of the race for the 1984 and 1986 data. This was done for two reasons. First, using the previous margin avoids the causality problem associated with using the final outcome of a race as the measure of closeness. This is especially critical when dealing with money in campaigns where the question arises as to whether or not the money was given to races that were close, or whether the contributions made the race close. Second, this type of information is part of what is available to decision makers in the legislative party campaign committees when they prepare to make their allocations. In fact, results from the telephone surveys indicated that a variation of the previous margin was among the factors many party committees used to determine which candidates to support.[1]

The specific measure for the previous margin is a folded scale using the candidate's party percentage in the previous election,[2] subtracting the absolute value of fifty minus the vote percentage from fifty: previous margin = 50− | 50 − previous vote percentage | . For the 1982 analysis, an average vote margin, calculated for the district using all three years was used as the measure of competitiveness of the district. Because Wisconsin was redistricted in 1982 and 1984, neither previous margins nor average margins could be used for those years, thus the only available measure of competition was the final outcome of the race. For this reason, caution in interpreting the results from Wisconsin is advised.

The use of the previous margin of victory is, at best, an imperfect surrogate for the closeness of the race.[3] Decision makers on the committees have additional information on which to base their decisions: polling, subjective impressions regarding the quality of their party's candidate and the quality of the opponent, and demographics research.[4] Such information is obviously unavailable to researchers and consequently is impossible to incorporate into the model. The inability to fully specify the model means the amount of variance explained will be relatively low. The conclusions derived from the analysis regarding the impact of the closeness of the race, and the willingness to fund nonincumbents should not, however, be affected by this problem because the error is on the conservative side. That is, if a relationship is found between a less-than-perfect indicator of the closeness of the race and the distribution of resources, a better measure would certainly produce a stronger relationship.[5]

Incumbency status was included in the regression in the form of a dummy variable that equaled 1 if the candidate was not an incumbent, and 0 if the candidate was an incumbent. This nonincumbent dummy variable allows for a test of the campaign committees' willingness to fund caucus outsiders. The actual regression model is as follows:

$$\text{CONTRIBUTION} = b_0 + b_1(\text{COMPETITION}) + b_2(\text{NONINC}) + e$$

where CONTRIBUTION is the level of assistance provided to a candidate from the legislative party campaign committee, in dollars, COMPETITION is the measure of competitiveness, and NONINC is the dummy variable for incumbency status. A second model was also run to take into consideration the fact that the relationship between the previous margin and contributions may not be linear, to examine the possibility that the levels of assistance increase at a greater rate as the perception of the competitiveness of the race reaches its highest levels. This analysis involved including the square of the measure of competitiveness in the equation.

If legislative party campaign committees' decisions are strategic, that is, if, as hypothesized, they concentrate resources on close races and are willing to fund nonincumbents, b_1 should be greater than zero and b_2 should be greater than or equal to zero. In other words, it is expected that the analysis will find a positive relationship between the closeness of the race and the level of assistance provided, and a positive relationship between the status as a nonincumbent and the level of assistance provided. If, on the other hand, the legislative party campaign committees follow conventional wisdom and restrict assistance to current members of the legislature, b_1 should be approximately zero and b_2 should be negative.

The limited number of cases in senate elections ruled out regression analysis. Instead, mean contributions were broken down by competitiveness and incumbency status. Because of the nature of senate races—running every four years, at the most—using previous vote margins or average votes as measures of competitiveness were not reasonable alternatives, leaving the final outcome as the only measure of closeness. This should be kept in mind while interpreting the results from the senate races.

House Legislative Party Campaign Committees

Table 5-1 presents the results of each of the regression analyses for all of the lower chamber campaign committees. Each line presents the results of a separate OLS regression analysis of model 5-1. Also included in the table are the mean contributions for each party committee—to provide a base of comparison between states—and the percent of the legislative seats held by the party prior to the election.

Legislative Caucus Campaign Committees. By studying the coefficients for the measure of competitiveness, we see that legislative party caucus campaign committees concentrate their resources on close races. Though the size of the coefficients vary, reflecting the varying levels of resources available to the caucus campaign committees, with one exception, every committee in every year provided a higher level of assistance as the competitiveness of the election increased.[6] That is, in fifty-three out of fifty-four cases the caucus campaign committees concentrated their resources on close races. The DFL caucus campaign committee in Minnesota in 1982, for example, gave, on average, an extra $8.40 for each tenth of a percent increase in the competitiveness of the district ($84.00 more for each 1 percent increase), while the IR caucus campaign committee provided $13.18 for each tenth of a percent increase in the competitiveness of the district (or $131.80 for each one percent increase). In California in 1986, for each tenth of a percent increase in the closeness of the previous margin, the California Assembly Democrats were likely to give an extra $2,371.16, the figure for the Republicans was $832.65.

This concentration of resources translates into high levels of assistance from the caucus campaign committees for some candidates. Jack Dugan, the Democratic candidate for the open California Assembly seat in District Five in the 1986 election received $589,171 from the Assembly Democrats (caucus committee), which was 67.4 percent of his total revenues! In the same year, challenger Johanna Willmann received $375,665, or 69 percent, of her total revenues from the Assembly Democrats in her bid for the seat of Assembly District Nine. In the 1986 contest for District Fifty-Six in Indiana—a contest that was decided by 5 votes—the Indiana House Democratic Caucus contributed $4,500 to the winning campaign of challenger Richard Bodiker, a small sum when compared to California contributions, but it constituted 43 percent of his total revenues. The House Republican Campaign Committee contributed $4,000 to the campaign of the district's incumbent Janet Hibner, which constituted 43 percent of her total revenues.

Because it is believed that the relationship between the competitiveness of the race and the amount of resources a caucus committee is willing to put into a race may increase at a greater rate as the races reach the highest levels of competitiveness, a nonlinear form of the regression model was tested. The results are presented in table 5-2 for the caucus campaign committees whose resource allocation pattern fits the nonlinear model.[7] Each of these cases represents a committee

Table 5-1. House Legislative Caucus Campaign Committee Expenditures Regressed upon Previous Margin and Incumbency

	Competi-tiveness*	Non-incumbent	Constant	R^2	N	% seats	Mean cont.
California							
D 1986	2371.16	48289.81	-55211.34	.18	76	59%	$33574
	(804.45)**	(22236.19)	(25676.40)				
R 1982	456.28	4012.24	-12301.34	.18	75	40%	$4844
	(138.12)	(2575.06)	(4590.88)				
R 1984	322.29	7984.81	-9935.24	.13	69	40%	$4635
	(124.56)	(3405.40)	(4735.62)				
R 1986	832.65	23968.72	-22356.06	.12	78	41%	$16323
	(367.82)	(10554.20)	(13198.36)				
Illinois							
D 1982	190.20	-2250.31	-931.96	.16	109	49%	$3410
	(43.40)	(1116.07)	(1433.73)				
D 1984	195.50	-1143.39	-1266.88	.24	112	59%	$3498
	(37.15)	(1196.70)	(1285.95)				
D 1986	122.97	-1378.09	1775.93	.10	107	57%	$4154
	(40.46)	(1475.33)	(1471.63)				
R 1982	125.01	-310.87	-1557.57	.21	97	51%	$1954
	(25.44)	(690.56)	(958.93)				
R 1984						41%	
R 1986	215.69	4109.23	-2936.07	.13	116	43%	$4754
	(63.55)	(2425.03)	(2340.16)				
Indiana							
D 1982	7.24	17.90	-97.52	.10	94	36%	$196
	(2.62)	(56.58)	(97.79)				
D 1984	14.59	-143.75	-17.47	.06	85	43%	$441
	(6.27)	(166.81)	(230.14)				
D 1986	36.62	925.11	-941.91	.17	86	39%	$1026
	(11.44)	(338.36)	(488.03)				
R 1982	27.68	-379.06	-323.93	.14	89	64%	$593
	(8.31)	(197.31)	(336.66)				
R 1984	12.93	-513.78	288.60	.16	97	57%	$591
	(5.72)	(174.91)	(252.35)				
R 1986	23.59	-159.50	74.60	.10	89	61%	$918
	(7.76)	(254.89)	(289.61)				
Minnesota							
D 1982	8.40	181.35	-143.72	.40	134	52%	$268
	(1.75)	(37.81)	(60.08)				
D 1984	18.64	518.95	-330.34	.31	128	57%	$596
	(4.08)	(110.99)	(152.43)				
D 1986	22.44	145.14	-543.42	.16	125	49%	$381
	(5.36)	(125.19)	(201.80)				
R 1982	13.18	114.98	-332.05	.20	121	48%	$241
	(2.57)	(47.33)	(108.52)				
R 1984	8.22	105.60	-154.51	.20	130	43%	$210
	(1.54)	(41.60)	(69.35)				
R 1986	9.81	150.16	-202.11	.14	123	51%	$242
	(2.50)	(59.82)	(105.02)				
Missouri							
D 1984	5.27	-52.00	117.44	.13	151	67%	$187
	(1.12)	(50.66)	(37.22)				
D 1986	12.44	-249.30	462.21	.10	142	66%	$550
	(3.38)	(137.14)	(85.24)				
R 1984	2.12	-64.23	29.84	.05	122	33%	$36
	(1.29)	(48.05)	(48.20)				
R 1986	3.49	41.35	79.17	.06	101	34%	$158
	(1.47)	(57.03)	(48.30)				
New York							
D 1984	328.47	8475.60	-3913.46	.20	138	65%	$5539
	(63.95)	(3305.05)	(1933.26)				
D 1986	487.73	3132.12	-7070.18	.28	138	63%	$6890
	(71.25)	(2098.14)	(2202.76)				

Continued on next page

Table 5-1—*Continued*

	Competi-tiveness*	Non-incumbent	Constant	R^2	N	% seats	Mean cont.
R 1984	165.22 (33.26)	4492.32 (1802.83)	-2219.23 (1037.19)	.19	143	35%	$2655
R 1986	333.91 (45.48)	1091.08 (1353.14)	-481.02 (1572.77)	.29	138	37%	$4620
Oregon							
D 1982	5.81 (4.45)	125.07 (77.31)	-174.39 (174.02)	.08	58	55%	$120
D 1984	-4.85 (8.48)	480.26 (137.87)	200.19 (354.18)	.21	56	60%	$286
D 1986	19.61 (11.89)	532.19 (402.64)	-210.01 (488.89)	.07	59	57%	$692
R 1982	17.02 (5.71)	394.89 (119.15)	-573.29 (223.64)	.28	59	45%	$306
R 1984	8.67 (24.97)	1711.29 (645.20)	-284.41 (970.84)	.13	54	40%	$1148
R 1986	5.80 (24.57)	2975.78 (794.18)	-176.49 (986.79)	.21	58	43%	$824
Tennessee							
D 1982	79.91 (14.50)	-554.45 (502.44)	477.65 (294.42)	.32	74	58%	$1600
D 1984	28.14 (12.17)	884.79 (464.17)	953.40 (312.38)	.12	79	62%	$1659
D 1986	21.41 (11.86)	1231.40 (465.40)	1037.82 (295.18)	.13	77	63%	$3101
R 1982	63.78 (12.01)	-1491.28 (377.57)	765.27 (294.92)	.36	55	40%	$1564
R 1984	19.07 (10.90)	-1393.25 (423.62)	2056.07 (331.24)	.20	57	38%	$1690
R 1986	13.64 (9.63)	-536.91 (392.42)	1374.55 (292.69)	.06	61	37%	$1757
Washington							
D 1982	19.72 (8.67)	61.53 (184.01)	-291.06 (306.92)	.07	98	43%	$480
D 1984	8.82 (16.21)	1111.52 (356.30)	-30.47 (645.77)	.10	99	55%	$977
D 1986	24.83 (9.84)	372.57 (200.37)	-612.27 (377.45)	.11	97	54%	$513
R 1982	63.98 (18.87)	586.59 (290.93)	-1890.64 (798.40)	.12	94	57%	$883
R 1984	29.56 (13.33)	1092.59 (287.21)	-1199.43 (606.85)	.15	95	45%	$620
R 1986	16.13 (11.11)	453.67 (203.11)	-480.27 (422.21)	.08	93	46%	$425
Wisconsin							
D 1982	40.81 (5.61)	58.58 (171.10)	-525.35 (189.42)	.42	98	60%	$891
D 1984	43.02 (6.69)	194.84 (191.75)	-674.13 (244.82)	.32	97	60%	$767
D 1986	28.27 (7.22)	346.81 (226.42)	-333.95 (233.28)	.24	84	53%	$709
R 1982	20.80 (5.65)	39.35 (123.73)	-338.58 (251.21)	.14	87	40%	$478
R 1984	17.64 (4.10)	31.17 (81.44)	-295.34 (137.78)	.22	86	40%	$342
R 1986	17.76 (5.03)	276.88 (146.59)	-259.72 (207.70)	.13	95	47%	$512

* The 1982 equations used average margin (calculated from the party's margin in 1982, 1984, and 1986) in lieu of previous margin. The 1982 and 1984 Wisconsin equations used the margin of victory in that year because of redistricting in the early 1980s.
** Figures in parentheses are the standard errors.

that concentrates its resources at a greater rate as the perceived competitiveness of the race increases. The coefficients are not as easily interpreted because their interpretation is tied to the level of the independent variable.[8] For example, for Illinois Democrats in 1986 an increase in the previous margin from 45 to 46 percent meant an additional $639.01 from the Illinois Democratic Majority Committee, while an increase from 49 to 50 percent meant an increase of $789.25.[9] Because the nonlinear form of the model is a better fit for these committees in these years—as indicated in part by the increased R-squares—this form of the model will be used throughout the rest of the book for these cases.

These results demonstrate a nearly universal pattern of concentration of resources in close races, providing overwhelming support of the first hypothesis among house legislative party caucus committees. The information gathered in the interviews corroborates these findings. When asked what criteria the committee uses in deciding which candidates to support, all of the responses, in one form of another, indicated that the competitiveness of the race was the main determining factor in deciding which candidates would receive support.

In addition to concentrating their resources in close races, it was posited that the goals pursued by caucus committees would lead them to support caucus outsiders, namely, nonincumbent candidates (hypothesis 2). Are legislative caucus campaign committees as willing to fund nonincumbents as incumbents? The answer to this question is found in tables 5-1 and 5-2. Counting the positive coefficients for nonincumbents (using the results from table 5-2 for those committees and the results from 5-1 for the others) forty-two of the fifty-seven committees (or 73.7 percent) were more likely to fund nonincumbent candidates, as reflected in the positive coefficients. In 1986 in Minnesota, for example, the mean contribution from the Democratic-Farmer-Labor House Caucus Committee was $93.05 (table 5-2) higher for nonincumbents (controlling for the closeness of the race). For Independent-Republican nonincumbent candidates, the mean contribution from their House Caucus Committee was $157.60 higher than for incumbents (also using table 5-2).

Of the fifteen negative results, eleven are found in states that have been traditionally dominated by one party—Indiana, Missouri, and Tennessee. These results are explained nicely by the hypothesized role played by party competition—hypothesis 3. In these states, the houses have long been dominated by one party—Republicans have dominated Indiana's house, and Democrats have dominated

Table 5-2. House Legislative Caucus Campaign Committee Expenditures Regressed upon Previous Margin, Previous Margin Squared, and Incumbency

	Competi-tiveness*	Compet. squared	Non-incumbent	Constant	R^2
California					
D 1986	-6364.94	193.34	58101.35	-3423.09	.34
	(2230.22)**	(46.67)	(20233.71)	(26356.40)	
R 1984	-843.29	24.19	10373.50	-2749.30	.24
	(378.13)	(7.65)	(3306.50)	(484860)	
Illinois					
D 1984	-467.72	15.12	-541.57	981.06	.43
	(118.25)	(2.59)	(1036.34)	(1173.33)	
D 1986	-389.69	12.03	-1882.91	3271.38	.19
	(163.12)	(3.72)	(1416.21)	(1473.07)	
R 1982	-167.05	5.75	104.02	789.25	.28
	(100.11)	(1.91)	(676.97)	(1206.91)	
R 1986	-277.04	11.79	4139.00	-1894.08	.16
	(259.70)	(6.03)	(2394.54)	(2371.35)	
Indiana					
D 1984	-71.86	1.88	-372.54	416.42	.23
	(21.24)	(.44)	(161.14)	(233.21)	
D 1986	-106.94	3.13	901.55	-449.29	.29
	(41.46)	(.87)	(316.35)	(476.40)	
R 1986	-30.75	1.13	-106.25	281.56	.14
	(27.78)	(.56)	(251.68)	(310.40)	
Minnesota					
D 1984	-29.47	.93	529.31	21.32	.38
	(13.65)	(.25)	(105.97)	(174.09)	
D 1986	-47.41	1.27	93.05	170.14	.27
R 1984	-6.38	.28	91.97	-33.80	.24
	(5.33)	(.10)	(40.74)	(79.60)	
R 1986	-17.26	.50	157.60	39.30	.22
Missouri					
D 1984	-8.54	.33	-71.71	148.09	.18
	(5.14)	(.12)	(49.94)	(37.98)	
R 1984	-8.67	.25	-60.90	52.83	.10
	(5.22)	(.12)	(47.06)	(48.40)	
New York					
D 1984	-713.69	20.64	8858.94	5424.07	.31
	(232.06)	(4.44)	(3078.20)	(2697.98)	
D 1986	-987.31	32.42	1033.30	3551.44	.50
	(200.42)	(4.21)	(1772.06)	(2297.57)	
R 1984	-170.32	6.74	5175.84	640.93	.23
	(126.60)	(2.45)	(1763.17)	(1453.77)	
R 1986	-791.95	24.79	1863.91	2023.93	.61
	(113.29)	(2.38)	(1010.77)	(1342.93)	
Oregon					
D 1986	-80.89	2.14	615.17	144.02	.16
	(43.89)	(.90)	(388.30)	(492.72)	
Washington					
D 1986	-47.58	1.28	473.97	129.32	.16
	(32.36)	(.55)	(200.42)	(485.88)	
R 1984	-119.00	2.50	1090.76	507.89	.24
	(43.64)	(.70)	(270.44)	(746.51)	
Wisconsin					
D 1982	-50.18	1.85	-68.98	-82.83	.57
	(16.15)	(.31)	(151.04)	(192.51)	
D 1984	-73.09	2.46	515.38	-120.04	.53
	(18.82)	(.38)	(167.68)	(221.80)	
D 1986	-50.81	1.72	364.66	54.28	.36
	(21.51)	(.44)	(208.98)	(237.52)	
R 1984	-14.03	.53	25.81	123.97	.27
	(13.93)	(.22)	(79.29)	(221.98)	
R 1986	-16.35	.73	256.44	-41.30	.18
	(15.25)	(.31)	(143.29)	(222.75)	

* The 1982 equations used average margin (calculated from the party's vote margin in the 1982, 1984, and 1986 elections) and average margin squared in lieu of previous margin.

** Figures in parentheses are the standard errors.

Tennessee's and Missouri's. Under conditions such as low levels of party competition, majority party status is no longer a top priority goal (mainly because it is less plausible), so a policy of contributing to nonincumbents would receive little or no support among caucus members. Furthermore, competition over districts is likely to be minimal, reducing the effectiveness of a strategy of supporting nonincumbents. Interparty competition cannot, however, explain the fact that the Illinois Democrats are less likely to fund nonincumbents; the level of competition is not as low as it is in Tennessee, Indiana, and Missouri. The one thing Illinois does share with the other three states is a large number of lopsided districts—the Chicago districts are strongholds of the Democrats and the suburban districts the stronghold of the Republicans, both with little real party competition. This type of apportionment means that in only a few cases will supporting a challenger, or even an open seat candidate, be a worthwhile endeavor. Though this is a seemingly plausible argument, it is contradicted by the fact that the Republicans in Illinois give greater emphasis to nonincumbent candidates and by the fact that caucus committees in New York, another state with many lopsided districts, are also more likely to fund nonincumbents. Consequently, the Illinois Democratic Majority Committee's emphasis on incumbents must be due to some other factor.

Thus, the regression results from the house legislative caucus campaign committees provides solid support for the argument that legislative party campaign committees strategically distribute their campaign resources. The notion that the caucus campaign committees focus their efforts on close races was overwhelmingly supported, and the notion that the caucus committees are willing to extend help to caucus outsiders because of the priority of the goal of majority status was also strongly supported.

A note of caution regarding conclusions about the funding of nonincumbents is, however, in order. The greater willingness to fund nonincumbents does not necessarily give us an indication of the priority given to such candidates by the campaign committees; it may be that few incumbents need help. In response to a question about supporting nonincumbents versus incumbents, the house caucus committees split roughly into two groups. A majority of the respondents indicated the caucus committee's number one priority was to protect incumbent candidates. The fact that the analysis does not reveal this priority is undoubtedly due to the simple fact that very few incumbents need help, because they have little trouble raising funds from other sources and benefit from the advantages of incumbency. The rest of the respondents indicated that the campaign committees supported candidates in close races regardless of whether they were incumbents. Some legislators and staff indicated that their senate caucus campaign committees actually avoided funding incumbent candidates. Thus, though a number of legislative party campaign committees' official policy is to protect incumbents first, the results of the analysis indicate that a substantial amount of their resources go to nonincumbent candidates.

Leadership PACs.   The regression results for the lower chamber legislative party leadership campaign committees (leadership PACs) are presented in table 5-3, with a format similar to the previous tables. As with the caucus campaign committees, considerable support is provided for the hypothesis that the committees concentrate their resources in close races.[10] In thirty-two out of the thirty-four cases the relationship between the closeness measure and the level of assistance is positive. Washington Democratic leadership PACs in 1986 were likely, on average, to give $52.77 more for each tenth of a percent increase in the previous margin (or $527.70 for each 1 percent increase), the figure for Washington Republicans was $30.15. The results from Wisconsin even when they are in the right direction are not very impressive. This is undoubtedly the result of the low level of this activity, a condition due to the state's strict campaign finance laws. In Wisconsin, leadership PACs are considered political action committees, and candidates who accept public funding are not allowed to accept contributions from PACs.[11]

Though leadership PAC contributions are usually less than those made by caucus campaign committees, this tendency to concentrate resources in close races can still result in substantial levels of assistance for particular candidates. For example, California incumbent Democrat Steve Clute from Assembly District Fifty-four received $62,000 in contributions from fifteen other legislators in 1986, a sum which constituted 25 percent of his total revenues. High levels of assistance can also be found in the states with smaller total contributions. An election in Washington illustrates this point. Brad Fisher, the Republican candidate for the second seat of District Sixteen received $7,563, or 12 percent of his total revenues, from fourteen other legislators.

The possibility that contributions from LPACs increase at a greater rate as the competitiveness of the race increases was tested in

Table 5-3. House Leadership PAC Expenditures Regressed upon Competitiveness and Incumbency

	Competi-tiveness*	Non-incumbent	Constant	R^2	N	Mean cont.
California						
D 1982	1746.17	2886.08	-17605.66	.03	75	$41844
	(1153.86)**	(20217.43)	(38728.52)			
D 1984	969.82	-24069.88	11057.59	.03	77	$34873
	(836.09)	(22721.77)	(30421.67)			
D 1986	638.01	5458.62	-10737.26	.19	76	$9636
	(170.27)	(4706.42)	(5434.56)			
R 1982	262.93	2311.39	-6866.05	.18	75	$3288
	(79.43)	(1480.92)	(2640.22)			
R 1984	523.57	10904.05	-13146.90	.12	71	$9335
	(213.48)	(5836.54)	(8116.42)			
R 1986	189.40	2690.08	-4386.32	.18	79	$2599
	(52.24)	(1499.03)	(1874.59)			
Minnesota						
D 1982	7.43	82.05	-124.87	.12	129	$210
	(2.62)	(56.01)	(90.99)			
D 1984	15.71	80.69	-106.44	.10	131	$513
	(4.51)	(122.73)	(168.55)			
D 1986	17.22	147.13	-405.54	.14	124	$325
	(4.58)	(106.88)	(172.29)			
R 1982	2.23	32.66	-27.71	.02	121	$78
	(1.63)	(30.19)	(69.05)			
R 1984	11.72	169.25	-328.72	.13	128	$208
	(2.88)	(77.84)	(129.80)			
R 1986	28.66	288.87	-693.79	.08	122	$491
	(9.12)	(218.35)	(383.32)			
Missouri						
D 1984	3.44	102.69	101.89	.04	151	$181
	(1.75)	(73.10)	(53.71)			
D 1986	1.69	36.20	247.05	.00	142	$281
	(5.41)	(219.31)	(136.31)			
R 1984	6.12	143.06	-115.37	.03	122	$88
	(4.55)	(170.21)	(170.74)			
R 1986	1.12	-40.64	73.98	.02	102	$72
	(1.17)	(45.67)	(38.68)			
Oregon						
D 1982	4.91	69.18	-156.45	.12	58	$71
	(2.40)	(41.74)	(93.95)			
D 1984	2.29	224.92	110.27	.04	55	$343
	(9.14)	(148.57)	(381.67)			
D 1986	24.83	11.65	176.87	.04	59	$988
	(15.63)	(528.22)	(641.36)			
R 1982	6.27	83.56	-169.75	.08	59	$114
	(3.51)	(73.26)	(137.50)			
R 1984	.68	166.83	-22.31	.12	53	$121
	(2.48)	(64.00)	(96.29)			
R 1986	7.66	141.64	-9.12	.03	57	$337
	(6.66)	(215.13)	(267.30)			
Washington						
D 1982	10.40	34.45	-183.08	.07	98	$232
	(4.46)	(96.75)	(161.37)			
D 1984	2.53	393.16	77.74	.06	98	$421
	(7.88)	(173.29)	(314.07)			
D 1986	52.77	730.86	-1241.50	.15	96	$1054
	(16.75)	(340.99)	(642.37)			
R 1982	4.19	112.17	-158.43	.04	95	$65
	(4.05)	(62.43)	(171.31)			
R 1984	7.25	200.93	-280.20	.06	95	$125
	(4.21)	(90.82)	(191.90)			
R 1986	30.15	438.16	-893.94	.08	92	$536
	(14.24)	(260.31)	(566.75)			
Wisconsin						
D 1982	-.84	-20.45	86.80	.02	98	$46
	(1.00)	(31.02)	(33.75)			

Continued on next page

Table 5-3—*Continued*

	Competi- tiveness*	Non- incumbent	Constant	R^2	N	Mean cont.
D 1984	-.40 (.76)	-16.77 (21.83)	65.76 (27.87)	.01	97	$38
D 1986	.40 (1.25)	1.87 (39.08)	40.68 (40.27)	.00	83	$53
R 1982	1.90 (1.01)	12.31 (22.10)	-49.59 (44.86)	.04	87	$97
R 1984	.83 (.84)	-4.47 (16.67)	-10.62 (28.20)	.01	86	$16
R 1986	.75 (1.41)	-81.57 (41.00)	63.64 (58.09)	.06	94	$47

* The 1982 equations used average margin (calculated from the party's margin in 1982, 1984, and 1986) in lieu of previous margin. The 1982 and 1984 Wisconsin equations used the margin of victory in that year because of redistricting in the early 1980s.
** Figures in parentheses are the standard errors.

the same manner as was done for the caucus campaign committees, by squaring the competitiveness measure and adding it to the equation. The results of this nonlinear regression are presented in table 5-4 for those groups of leadership PACs that fit the model.[12] For the cases appearing in this table, the nonlinear form of the regression model constitutes the best fit and therefore will be used throughout the rest of the book.

According to the OLS coefficients, leadership PACs were also more likely to contribute to the campaigns of nonincumbents. In twenty-eight out of the thirty-four cases the coefficient for the nonincumbent variable is positive. A DFL nonincumbent candidate in the 1986 elections in Minnesota was likely to receive an average $103.44 more than incumbent candidates from leadership PACs, controlling for the closeness of the race (table 5-4). Independent-Republican leaders were likely to give on average $307.07 more to nonincumbents, controlling for the closeness of the race (also from table 5-4). Wisconsin accounts for four of the five negative results, a finding that is once again undoubtedly due to the small amount of money involved in Wisconsin.

Missouri Democratic leadership PACs were more likely to fund nonincumbents than their caucus committee (see table 5-1). This anomaly contradicts expectations—the leaders' behavior suggests greater concern with party interests than the House Democratic Campaign Committee—and thus demands explanation. The reason can be found in the discussion of the operation of the House Democratic Campaign Committee in chapter 4. The HDCC collects contributions from incumbents and returns the contributions to them at election time. In this way it has acted much like an incumbent trust fund, especially in its earliest years—1984 and 1986. The lack of a strong chal-

Table 5-4. House Leadership PAC Expenditures Regressed upon Competitiveness, Competitiveness Squared, and Incumbency

	Competi- tiveness*	Compet. squared	Non- incumbent	Constant	R^2
California					
D 1984	-4882.11	123.05	-32214.95	54327.96	.10
	(2642.36)**	(52.87)	(22348.95)		
D 1986	-1209.62	40.89	7533.94	216.88	.35
	(472.11)	(9.88)	(4283.26)		
R 1982	-563.16	13.61	2776.33	4326.71	.22
	(410.59)	(6.64)	(1466.74)		
R 1984	-1394.35	40.79	15342.29	-2879.19	.23
	(649.62)	(13.14)	(5680.50)		
R 1986	-295.96	11.26	1380.76	-815.63	.29
	(151.43)	(3.33)	(1457.53)		
Minnesota					
D 1984	-35.48	.99	91.71	267.79	.18
	(15.15)	(.28)	(117.63)		
D 1986	-41.37	1.07	103.44	192.94	.25
	(14.63)	(.25)	(100.79)		
R 1984	-15.91	.53	141.74	-102.62	.18
	(10.00)	(.18)	(76.27)		
R 1986	-37.66	1.23	307.07	-102.34	.12
	(30.56)	(.54)	(214.79)		
Oregon					
D 1986	-124.27	3.18	134.76	702.13	.16
	(56.74)	(1.17)	(501.93)	(636.93)	
Washington					
D 1986	-96.36	2.64	939.71	285.99	.22
	(54.31)	(.92)	(336.33)	(815.34)	
Wisconsin					
D 1984	-5.22	.10	-3.46	88.75	.05
	(2.53)	(.05)	(22.50)	(29.76)	

* The 1982 equations used average margin (calculated from the party's vote margin in the 1982, 1984, and 1986 elections) and average margin squared in lieu of previous margin.
** Figures in parentheses are standard errors.

lenge by Republicans in the state probably had a role in the way that this practice developed, that is, the goal of majority party status was secure, so there was little need to fund caucus outsiders. So, while the HDCC was run like an incumbent trust fund, its emphasis was on incumbents. Why leadership PACs emphasize nonincumbents in this state lacking in party competition must be related to the practices of the HDCC. With the HDCC funding incumbents, leadership PACs must see a greater opportunity to have an effect by funding nonincumbents.

Thus, both types of house legislative party campaign committees have been found to concentrate their resources in close races and to provide greater assistance to nonincumbent candidates. For comparison, the results for a number of the state party organizations are shown in table 5-5. These results illustrate a considerably poorer showing on the part of some of the state party organizations in the utilization of their campaign resources in legislative elections. This is

Table 5-5. State Central Committee Expenditures Regressed upon Previous Margin and Incumbency

	Previous margin*	Nonincumbent	Constant	R^2
California				
Democrats 1982	-8.61	-2087.78	2559.73	.02
Democrats 1984	-12.52	802.97	510.22	.07
Democrats 1986	26.12	613.00	-317.31	.03
Republicans 1982	579.11	9774.64	-16764.27	.21
Republicans 1984	203.42	8366.55	-5049.07	.11
Republicans 1986	183.37	4206.33	-4674.65	.10
Minnesota				
Democrats 1982	-1.02	7.28	52.19	.00
Democrats 1984	.17	1.22	-4.20	.01
Democrats 1986		none		
Republicans 1982	25.81	201.65	-563.61	.19
Republicans 1984	20.35	233.29	-160.02	.16
Republicans 1986	6.18	205.04	-192.68	.12
Oregon				
Democrats 1982	1.49	36.16	-54.92	.03
Democrats 1984	2.15	145.19	-87.43	.07
Democrats 1986	1.50	-49.47	2.50	.03
Republicans 1982	-2.07	-58.74	148.71	.03
Republicans 1984	3.12	646.14	-124.14	.13
Republicans 1986	-7.34	981.89	242.08	.09
Washington				
Democrats 1982	35.53	-148.73	-620.82	.06
Democrats 1984	20.94	202.72	-144.71	.02
Democrats 1986	19.86	904.16	-462.81	.08
Republicans 1982	64.20	85.66	-1304.97	.04
Republicans 1984	105.78	3051.85	-4462.05	.22
Republicans 1986	24.69	967.37	-856.85	.09
Wisconsin				
Democrats 1982	6.84	-11.19	-166.89	.12
Democrats 1984	2.04	-19.53	-32.21	.06
Democrats 1986	4.33	-51.85	-40.05	.02
Republicans 1982	.27	.74	17.19	.00
Republicans 1984	38.83	-87.08	-976.31	.28
Republicans 1986	11.27	142.78	-103.69	.08

* The 1982 equations used average margin (calculated from the party's margin in 1982, 1984, and 1986) in lieu of previous margin. The 1982 and 1984 Wisconsin equations used the margin of victory in that year because of redistricting in the early 1980s.

especially the case for the state Democratic parties, which showed little evidence of concentrating their resources on close races and did not give any preference to nonincumbent candidates. The Democratic legislative parties turn out to be much more efficient than their state organizations. The poor showing of the state parties may be explained by the low levels of assistance most of them provide, a finding significant in and of itself, because it demonstrates that in these cases the dominant party actor in legislative elections has become the legislative party, probably formed to fill a void left by the party, as argued in chapter 1. The stronger showing by Republican state parties is undoubtedly related to the superior organizational strength and resources of the Republican parties at the state level.[13]

Senate Legislative Party Campaign Committees

Analysis of the senate party campaign committees was conducted using a simple breakdown of the assistance provided by the committees in lieu of regression because of the small number of cases in most senate elections. Though this form of analysis may lack the sophistication of regression, it still provides ample means to test the hypotheses regarding the distributional strategy of legislative party campaign committees. The limited availability of the previous margin for senate districts (because senate races are held every four years and redistricting occurred after the 1980 election) means that the final outcome of the race had to be used as the measure of closeness. Because of this, special caution must be taken in the interpretation of the senate campaign committee results.

Senate Caucus Campaign Committees.   The mean contributions received by incumbents and nonincumbents in competitive and noncompetitive races from senate caucus campaign committees for 1982 through 1986 are shown in table 5-6. The table includes the means broken down by incumbency and competitiveness, the number of candidates fitting into each category (in parentheses), and the ratios of the mean contributions of candidates in competitive races to those in noncompetitive races, and of nonincumbents in competitive races to incumbents in competitive races. A race was considered competitive if the winning candidate received less than 60 percent of the vote and the losing candidate received more than 40 percent of the vote.

Just as their house counterparts, most of the senate caucus campaign committees concentrate their resources on close races. Looking at the means and the ratio of the mean contributions received by candidates in competitive races to those in noncompetitive races, it is evident that candidates in competitive races receive, on average, a larger contribution from the senate caucus campaign committees. California Republicans in 1982, for example, spent all of their resources on candidates that received between 40 and 60 percent of the vote. Washington Democrats in 1984 spent an average of $5,640 on nonincumbents in competitive races and $4,905 on incumbents in close races, while spending an average of $1,016 and $296 on nonincumbents and incumbents in races where the winning candidate received sixty percent or more of the vote—a ratio of 7.64 to 1. Minnesota Democrats in 1986 spent an average of $3,163 and $3,153 on nonincumbents and incumbents in close races, while spending an average of only $463 and $198 on nonincumbents and incumbents in races that were not close—a ratio of 10.73 to 1. The Illinois Republicans' average contribution to competitive candidates was 333 times greater than their average contribution to candidates in noncompetitive races. In total, in forty out of forty-eight cases the ratio of the average contributions to candidates in competitive races was at least two times greater than those in noncompetitive races.

As with house races, the targeting of resources by the caucus committees means that selected candidates will receive rather large sums from the legislative party. The 1986 open seat race for the Thirty-fifth Senate District in New York provides a good illustration. The Republican candidate, Nicholas Spano, received $313,216 from the senate Republican caucus committee, while the Democrat, Andrew MacDonald, received $185,785 from the Democratic caucus! MacDonald won with 46.9 percent of the vote. Of the $1,058,074 raised by challenger Tom Legan in the race for the Twelfth Senate District in California, $372,192 came from the Senate Republican PAC; that is, he received 35.2 percent of his total revenues from the senate Republican caucus campaign committee.

A few senate caucus campaign committees did not appear to be very efficient in terms of focusing on close races—the Tennessee Democratic and Wisconsin Republican committees. In Tennessee, this is, in large part, because of the lack of candidates in close races, which is a result of the low party competition in that state. This finding provides further evidence in support for hypothesis 3.

Are senate caucus campaign committees willing to fund nonincumbent candidates as their house counterparts do? The answer is yes—every committee that had nonincumbent candidates in close races devoted some of their resources to those races. Almost all of the committees were also willing to contribute their resources to nonincumbent candidates in races that ended up being not so close. And, finally, twenty-eight of the forty-two cases for which a ratio could be calculated, the ratio of the mean for nonincumbents in competitive races to the mean of nonincumbents in close races was greater than one, indicating that these caucus committees actually gave greater emphasis to nonincumbent candidates.[14] In five of the six cases where no incumbents were in close races—the California Republicans in 1984 and 1986, the Tennessee Democrats in 1982, and the Tennessee Republicans in 1984 and 1986—the mean contributions for nonincumbents in both competitive and noncompetitive races is clearly greater than the average contribution received by the incumbents, a result

Table 5-6. Distribution of Senate Caucus Campaign Committee Contributions in 1982-1986 with Means, and Number of Cases Broken Down by Incumbency and Competitiveness*

	Nonincumbents		Incumbents		Comp/	Noninc/
	Comp	Noncomp	Comp	Noncomp	Ncomp*	Inc
California						
D 1986	12500(2)	0(0)	20867(2)	2083(12)	8.01	0.60
R 1982	4330(5)	0(9)	27684(2)	0(2)	+**	0.16
R 1984	105333(3)	278(9)	0(0)	5000(8)	42.13	--
R 1986	213124(3)	15009(12)	0(0)	0(4)	18.93	--
Illinois						
D 1982	1875(4)	838(16)	2150(5)	550(19)	2.97	0.87
D 1984	3500(1)	2458(6)	10083(3)	694(7)	5.59	0.35
D 1986	33459(2)	250(2)	27943(3)	1728(17)	19.17	1.20
R 1982	19356(6)	174(10)	12708(4)	3644(16)	7.23	1.52
R 1984	59489(3)	0(1)	9193(1)	3446(7)	15.56	6.47
R 1986	153013(3)	287(14)	73938(2)	485(9)	333.03	2.07
Indiana						
D 1982	432(11)	313(4)	2250(2)	550(5)	1.60	0.19
D 1984	957(2)	0(10)	0(0)	942(5)	3.05	--
D 1986	3275(6)	0(6)	1500(2)	0(5)	+	2.18
R 1982	1083(6)	458(6)	4393(7)	1133(3)	4.20	0.25
R 1984	3500(1)	180(5)	4083(6)	1475(10)	3.83	0.86
R 1986	6375(4)	542(6)	6833(3)	5375(4)	2.65	0.93
Minnesota						
D 1982	1451(22)	381(9)	499(10)	96(24)	6.64	2.91
D 1986	3163(12)	463(16)	3153(9)	198(28)	10.73	1.00
R 1982	606(20)	189(9)	420(10)	79(23)	4.95	1.44
R 1986	2777(14)	814(26)	2340(7)	437(13)	3.82	1.19
New York						
D 1984	58562(5)	627(32)	11063(3)	0(3)	71.08	5.29
D 1986	137211(3)	1987(24)	68596(3)	0(23)	101.42	2.00
R 1984	143578(3)	4384(19)	11204(12)	1993(21)	12.04	12.81
R 1986	228747(3)	10914(18)	67639(10)	1845(18)	16.43	3.38
Oregon						
D 1982	774(7)	50(2)	800(2)	133(3)	7.81	0.97
D 1984	488(4)	200(5)	417(3)	0(3)	3.66	1.17
D 1986	3848(3)	417(3)	1188(4)	1825(4)	1.91	3.24
R 1982	1483(6)	217(6)	567(3)	0(0)	5.43	2.62
R 1984	774(7)	50(2)	800(2)	133(3)	7.81	0.97
R 1986	5219(5)	5256(5)	420(2)	0(2)	1.02	12.43
Tennessee						
D 1982	5125(4)	2667(4)	0(0)	2833(6)	1.85	--
D 1984	5500(2)	2000(5)	8000(1)	6857(7)	1.31	0.69
D 1986	2000(4)	0(0)	7250(4)	3000(6)	1.54	0.28
R 1982	6333(3)	3000(1)	5000(1)	857(7)	5.33	1.27
R 1984	12500(3)	0(1)	0(0)	3333(3)	5.00	--
R 1986	9000(8)	0(1)	0(0)	0(2)	+	--
Washington						
D 1982	4640(10)	481(3)	6819(1)	257(6)	14.59	0.68
D 1984	5640(10)	1016(7)	4905(3)	296(5)	7.64	1.15
D 1986	7191(7)	1650(5)	6444(2)	450(8)	7.71	1.12

Continued on next page

Table 5-6—*Continued*

	Nonincumbents		Incumbents		Comp/ Ncomp	Noninc/ Inc
	Comp	Noncomp	Comp	Noncomp		
R 1982	3726(5)	702(8)	2094(6)	0(1)	4.54	1.78
R 1984	5617(6)	1137(7)	1304(7)	329(5)	4.12	4.12
R 1986	19523(5)	1854(9)	819(4)	1463(4)	6.47	6.47
Wisconsin						
D 1982	5321(7)	875(4)	5900(1)	2525(4)	3.17	3.17
D 1984	5615(5)	1092(5)	2473(3)	6000(1)	2.32	2.32
D 1986	6489(2)	3104(7)	3325(2)	1177(6)	2.22	2.22
R 1982	1516(3)	1386(4)	2500(5)	1075(2)	1.66	1.66
R 1984	2599(3)	1464(6)	850(4)	100(1)	1.26	1.26
R 1986	7105(3)	1936(6)	3220(1)	2281(6)	2.91	2.91

* Competitive is defined as being within the 40-60% vote range.
** A + represents cases with a division by zero but with an $\underline{N}$ greater than 0; -- represents cases with a division by zero and with a zero $\underline{N}$.

that also suggests that a greater emphasis is given to nonincumbents by these committees.

The results of the interviews supplement the conclusions drawn from the data regarding the concentration of resources. All respondents from senate caucus campaign committees stated that their committee tends to target its resources, giving to races that appear to be competitive.

As with the house caucus campaign committees, some of the responses given in the interviews contradict the second finding, that is, that emphasis is placed on funding nonincumbents. Eleven out of seventeen respondents for senate caucus campaign committees indicated that incumbents were the number one priority. The reason for this was best stated by Indiana minority leader Dennis Neary, who said that Democrats in the senate "don't want to lose any seats we already have." Why is this preference for incumbents not reflected in the actual distribution of assistance? It is probably, once again, because of the fact that the dominant criteria used by all committees is the funding of candidates in competitive or close races, and the fact that most incumbents do not find themselves in that situation. This is supported by the fact that the contacts from all of these committees indicated that after all incumbents are taken care of the caucus committee focuses its attention on open seat races and challengers. As Bob Haggerty, executive director of the Senate Republican Campaign Committee (SRCC) in New York, put it, "[SRCC assistance] goes first to incumbents who need assistance—the number one priority is to maintain the majority—and then we look at other viable races."

Thus, the senate party caucus campaign committee results provide additional evidence that legislative party caucus campaign committees concentrate their resources on close races and are willing to fund nonincumbents as well as incumbents. As a consequence of this strategic behavior, the impact caucus campaign committees have on legislative elections and legislative behavior is maximized.

Senate Leadership PACs.   Table 5-7 contains the mean contributions for the senate leadership PACs broken down by incumbency and competitiveness and the ratio of the average contribution received by candidates in competitive races to those in noncompetitive races.

According to the ratio of the average contributions received by candidates in competitive races to those in noncompetitive races, it appears that senate leadership PACs concentrate their resources on close races. In twenty-two out of twenty-eight cases the ratio is greater than one. Among the groups of leaders who seemed to be concentrating their resources are the California Democrats, who, in 1982 contributed an average of $97,962 and $109,167 to nonincumbents and incumbents in races that were decided by less than a 60/40 percent margin, compared to an average of $2,063 for nonincumbents and $600 for incumbents in contests that were decided by a margin greater than 60/40, a ratio of 76.73 to 1. The state where the leadership PACs appeared to be the least efficient in contributing to competitive races is Wisconsin. This is because of the small amounts of money involved as a result of strict campaign finance laws that effectively discourage leadership PACs.

All leadership groups, with the exception of the Wisconsin Democrats in 1986, contributed some money to nonincumbent candidates. The ratio of mean contributions indicates that in eighteen out of the twenty eight cases nonincumbents in close races were given a greater priority than incumbents in close races. In Oregon, for example, nonincumbent Democratic candidates in close races in 1984 averaged contributions of $913 from Democratic leadership PACs while incumbents in close races averaged $167, a ratio of 5.47 to 1. It appears that senate leadership PACs, like their house counterparts, target their resources, focusing on close races with a willingness to fund nonincumbent candidates. Though the cases for the senate caucus campaign committees and leadership PACs were much smaller than those for the house committees, evidence of the tendency to strategically utilize their resources held across three years for most committees.

Table 5-7. Distribution of Leadership PAC Contributions in 1982-1986 Senate Races with Means, and Number of Cases Broken Down by Incumbency and Competitiveness*

	Nonincumbents		Incumbents		Comp/	Noninc/
	Comp	Noncomp	Comp	Noncomp	Ncomp*	Inc
California						
D 1982	97962(5)	2063(5)	109167(3)	600(5)	76.73	0.90
D 1984	68943(1)	4505(10)	37500(1)	5763(8)	10.51	1.84
D 1986	615000(2)	39667(3)	302339(3)	38938(12)	10.94	2.03
R 1982	28944(5)	1278(9)	57250(2)	5000(2)	18.94	0.51
R 1984	42667(3)	0(9)	0(0)	188(8)	482.27	--**
R 1986	112641(3)	8848(12)	0(0)	1375(4)	16.14	--
Minnesota						
D 1982	606(20)	189(9)	420(10)	79(23)	4.95	1.44
D 1986	3547(12)	628(16)	3061(9)	493(28)	6.16	1.16
R 1982	125(19)	123(23)	133(10)	0(7)	1.35	0.94
R 1986	2511(14)	156(26)	564(7)	0(13)	17.90	4.45
Oregon						
D 1982	343(7)	0(2)	0(2)	0(3)	+	+
D 1984	913(4)	327(5)	167(3)	0(3)	2.90	5.47
D 1986	267(3)	100(3)	100(4)	50(4)	2.40	2.67
R 1982	63(6)	0(6)	33(3)	0(0)	+	1.91
R 1984	270(5)	0(3)	0(2)	0(3)	+	+
R 1986	343(5)	662(5)	0(2)	0(2)	0.52	+
Washington						
D 1982	846(10)	0(3)	0(1)	179(6)	6.44	+
D 1984	505(10)	143(7)	183(3)	65(5)	3.90	2.76
D 1986	4221(7)	340(6)	6375(2)	163(8)	20.34	0.66
R 1982	250(5)	0(8)	0(6)	0(1)	+	+
R 1984	233(6)	0(7)	200(7)	0(5)	+	1.17
R 1986	4860(5)	694(4)	0(4)	0(4)	7.78	+
Wisconsin						
D 1982	32(7)	361(4)	100(1)	20(4)	0.21	0.32
D 1984	8(5)	23(5)	0(3)	0(1)	0.26	+
D 1986	0(2)	0(7)	220(2)	28(6)	8.51	0.00
R 1982	212(3)	22(4)	342(5)	250(2)	2.99	0.62
R 1984	21(3)	37(6)	4(4)	0(1)	0.36	5.25
R 1986	172(3)	0(6)	0(1)	0(6)	+	+

* Competitive is defined as being within the 40-60% vote range.
** A + represents cases with a division by zero but with an N greater than 0; -- represents cases with a division by zero and with a zero N.

Conclusion

In summary, the results of the analysis of house and senate party caucus campaign committees and leadership PACs provide substantial support for the hypothesized behavior of legislative party campaign committees. Legislative party campaign committees concentrate their resources in close races, whether or not that means supporting an incumbent. The extent to which they act strategically appears to be affected by the level of interparty competition that exists within the state or the districts. In the states in the sample with low levels of interparty competition, the campaign committees still concentrated their resources in close races, but were less likely to fund nonincumbents.

By concentrating their resources on competitive races and by funding caucus outsiders, legislative party campaign committees are maximizing the effect they have on legislative elections and consequently on legislative behavior. Legislative party campaign committees, especially the caucus campaign committees, are playing a role in legislative politics that far exceeds the picture one gets from looking just at their total expenditures. While these committees usually constitute less than 10 percent of all the revenues raised in the state legislative elections, their practices extend their influence far beyond their resources. They have a great deal of influence on the decisions of other contributors. They provide services that they can purchase at a bulk discount, passing on the savings to their candidates. They perform party-type services—recruitment and voter mobilization. They redistribute campaign funds and concentrate their valuable resources and energy in competitive races, maximizing the effect their efforts will have on the outcome of elections and consequently the makeup of state legislatures. Legislative party campaign committees have become, or are in the process of becoming, major actors in state legislative politics, a development with repercussions for legislative behavior, state party systems, public policy, and campaign finance. Having thus established the importance of these committees, the next two chapters look into the possible differences that may exist between the two types of legislative party campaign committees—caucus committees and leadership PACs—and into possible variations in campaign committee strategies.

6

Caucus Campaign Committees Versus Leadership PACs

Clearly, legislative caucus campaign committees and legislative leadership PACs are two distinct types of organizations. Caucus campaign committees operate much like political parties, representing in theory, if not in fact, all of the legislative party members. Leadership PACs, on the other hand, consist solely of an individual legislator's own campaign funds. On the surface, the differences between these two types of committees might lead one to expect that they would act very differently from each other in distributing their resources. The theoretical arguments made in the second chapter, however, suggest that under high levels of two-party competition the goals of those in charge of both leadership PACs and caucus committees converge, leading to an expectation that both committees would behave similarly with one exception, namely, the level of assistance extended to nonincumbent candidates. The purpose of this chapter is to test the hypothesized similarities and differences in resource allocation between legislative party caucus campaign committees and legislative leadership PACs.

Because it is assumed that those in control of leadership PACs are no less rational than those in control of the caucus committees, leadership PACs should distribute their limited resources in such a way as to have the greatest impact. In legislative elections this means concentrating those resources on competitive races where marginal value of each dollar is much greater than in races that lack serious competition. Because this is the same strategy followed by caucus campaign committees, no difference is expected between the two types of committees in terms of concentrating resources in marginal races.

On the other hand, a difference is expected between leadership PACs and caucus campaign committees in their willingness to fund nonincumbent candidates, for two reasons. First, for those vying for leadership posts, incumbents represent a better return on a campaign contribution investment, that is, they have a very high reelection success rate, so they are likely to be a member of the caucus following the election. Second, party control of the legislature is not as high a priority goal for legislators as it is for the party caucus: more important is a legislator's own career advancement, which can be enhanced by contributing to the campaigns of those who select the party leaders, that is, other caucus members.

The hypotheses that will be tested are:

4. Legislative leadership PACs should be as efficient at concentrating their resources on close races as caucus campaign committees in states with high levels of interparty competition.
5. Leadership PACs should be less likely to fund nonincumbent candidates than caucus campaign committees.

Method

To achieve the comparability necessary to test these hypotheses, a new set of regressions were run on the campaign contributions data for the house races in each of the three years. The dependent variable in the previous regression model was changed from the actual dollar level of assistance received by a candidate to the proportion of all of the committee's funds that a candidate received. This provides results regarding the relative distribution of the committees' resources. It also provides results that are comparable because the coefficients represent the emphasis committees put on types of candidates regardless of the actual amount of money campaign committees have to distribute. The rest of the regression model is the same as used before:

$$PROPLPCC = b_0 + b_1(COMPETITION) + b_2(COMPETITION)^2 + b_3(NONINC) + e$$

where PROPLPCC is the proportion of the committee funds going to an individual candidate, COMPETITION is the measure of the competitiveness of the race (the previous margin for 1984 and 1986, and the average margin for 1982), COMPETITION^2 is the square of the competitiveness measure (included only if it represented a better model of the relationship—see chapter 5), and NONINC is the dummy variable for incumbency (equaling 0 if the candidate is an incumbent, and 1 if the candidate is not an incumbent).

In addition to separate regression runs for each caucus campaign committee and leadership PAC, a set of regressions were run on a pooled data set containing candidate records from all six states for which both caucus campaign committee and leadership PAC data were available. One regression was run for each party in each year. This was done to allow for an overall comparison of caucus campaign committees and leadership PACs. Besides the measures of competitiveness and incumbency status, dummy variables for each state were incorporated into the model to control for any state to state variation in resource allocation. The exact regression model used in the analysis was:

$$\text{PROPLPCC} = b_0 + b_1(\text{COMPET}) + b_2(\text{COMPET})^2 + b_3(\text{NONINC}) \\ + b_4(\text{CALIFORNIA}) + \ldots + b_8(\text{WASHINGTON}) + e$$

where the first three variables are the same as in equation 6-1, and CALIFORNIA through WASHINGTON are dummy variables for five of the six states used in the comparison.[1] Including dummy variables for each state also makes it possible to include the squared term even though it is important for only some committees (see Chapter 5).[2]

Results

The results of the regressions for each committee and for the pooled data are presented in table 6-1. Focusing first on the individual states: as expected, there seems to be little evidence of a difference in the targeting of competitive races between caucus campaign committees and leadership PACs. For most cases the coefficients for the competitiveness measure(s) are very similar.[3] The Oregon Republicans in 1982, for example, had a caucus campaign committee that distributed an average of .95 percent more of their resources to a candidate for each percent increase in the competitiveness of the race (.095 percent for each tenth of a percent increase), while their leadership PACs distributed .93 percent more of their resources for each one percent increase in the competitiveness of the race. Moreover, where the committees do differ in concentrating on competitive races, the committee that targets close races better is not always the caucus campaign committee. To illustrate, in 1986 the Missouri Democrats' caucus committee

Table 6-1. Caucus Campaign Committees and Leadership PACs Compared*

	1982		1984		1986	
	LCC	LPACS	LCC	LPACS	LCC	LPACS
California Democrats						
competitiveness					-.253	-.167
					(.089)	(.065)
comp. squared	no		no		.007	.006
					(.002)	(.001)
nonincumbent	caucus		caucus		2.307	1.042
					(.804)	(.592)
constant	committee		committee		-.136	.030
					(1.047)	(.772)
R-square					.34	.35
California Republicans						
competitiveness	.126	-.249	-.256	-.213	.066	-.148
	(.038)	(.181)	(.115)	(.099)	(.029)	(.076)
comp. squared		.006	.007	.006		.006
		(.002)	(.002)	(.002)		(.002)
nonincumbent	1.104	1.229	3.152	2.343	1.907	.690
	(.709)	(.649)	(1.005)	(.868)	(.840)	(.728)
constant	-3.386	1.915	-.836	-.440	-1.779	-.408
	(1.264)	(2.674)	(1.474)	(1.272)	(1.050)	(1.024)
R-square	.18	.22	.24	.23	.12	.29
Minnesota Democrats						
competitiveness	.023	.028	-.038	-.054	-.105	-.107
	(.004)	(.010)	(.017)	(.023)	(.038)	(.038)
comp. squared			.001	.002	.003	.003
			(.0004)	(.0004)	(.0007)	(.0007)
nonincumbent	.505	.316	.678	.141	.208	.269
	(.105)	(.215)	(.136)	(.181)	(.261)	(.262)
constant	-.400	-.480	.027	.411	.378	.501
	(.167)	(.350)	(.223)	(.300)	(.560)	(.560)
R-square	.39	.12	.18	.18	.27	.25
Minnesota Republicans						
competitiveness	.045	.024	-.024	-.061	-.061	-.062
	(.009)	(.018)	(.020)	(.039)	(.029)	(.050)
comp. squared			.001	.002	.002	.002
			(.0004)	(.0007)	(.0005)	(.0009)
nonincumbent	.390	.351	.339	.546	.557	.505
	(.161)	(.324)	(.150)	(.294)	(.202)	(.353)
constant	-1.128	-.298	-.125	-.395	.139	-.168
	(.368)	(.742)	(.294)	(.573)	(.431)	(.754)
R-square	.20	.02	.24	.18	.22	.12
Missouri Democrats						
competitiveness			-.030	.013	.016	.004
			(.018)	(.006)	(.004)	(.013)
comp. squared	no		.001			
			(.0004)			
nonincumbent	no		-.253	.375	-.319	.091
			(.176)	(.267)	(.176)	(.549)
constant	caucus		.522	.373	.592	.619
			(.134)	(.196)	(.109)	(.341)
R-square	committee		.18	.04	.10	.001
Missouri Republicans						
competitiveness			-.197	.057	.028	.015
			(.119)	(.042)	(.011)	(.016)
comp. squared	no		.006			
			(.0027)			
nonincumbent	caucus		-1.384	1.331	.331	-.555
			(1.069)	(1.584)	(.456)	(.624)

Continued on next page

*Unstandardized regression coefficients resulting from regressing the proportion of committee funds received by a candidate upon the competitive measures and a dummy variable for incumbency status.

Table 6-1—*Continued*

	1982		1984		1986	
	LCC	LPACS	**LCC**	**LPACS**	LCC	LPACS
constant	committee		1.200	-1.074	.633	1.011
			(1.100)	(1.589)	(.386)	(.529)
R-square			.10	.03	.06	.02
Oregon Democrats						
competitiveness	.085	.122	-.012	.004	-.202	-.217
	(.065)	(.060)	(.021)	(.016)	(.109)	(.099)
comp. squared					.005	.006
					(.002)	(.002)
nonincumbent	1.829	1.719	1.197	.393	1.547	.235
	(1.130)	(1.037)	(.344)	(.259)	(.968)	(.867)
constant	-2.551	-3.889	.499	.193	.359	1.226
	(2.545)	(2.335)	(.883)	(.666)	(1.228)	(1.112)
R-square	.08	.12	.21	.04	.16	.16
Oregon Republicans						
competitiveness	.095	.093	.008	.004	.006	.041
	(.031)	(.052)	(.024)	(.013)	(.024)	(.035)
nonincumbent	2.190	1.242	1.675	.884	2.913	.751
	(.661)	(1.089)	(.632)	(.339)	(.777)	(1.140)
constant	-3.179	-2.523	-.278	-.118	-.173	-.048
	(1.240)	(2.044)	(.950)	(.510)	(.966)	(1.416)
R-square	.28	.08	.13	.12	.21	.03
Washington Democrats						
competitiveness	.042	.169	.009	.022	-.103	-.095
	(.018)	(.074)	(.017)	(.067)	(.070)	(.053)
comp. squared					.003	.003
					(.001)	(.0009)
nonincumbent	.131	.560	1.172	3.335	1.024	.928
	(.391)	(1.573)	(.376)	(1.470)	(.433)	(.332)
constant	-.619	-2.977	-.032	.660	.298	.283
	(.652)	(2.623)	(.681)	(2.665)	(1.050)	(.805)
R-square	.07	.07	.10	.06	.16	.22
Washington Republicans						
competitiveness	.077	.092	-.204	.010	.041	.061
	(.023)	(.089)	(.075)	(.005)	(.028)	(.029)
comp. squared			.004			
			(.001)			
nonincumbent	.707	2.478	1.872	.266	1.159	.888
	(.351)	(1.379)	(.464)	(.120)	(.519)	(.528)
constant	-2.278	-3.500	.872	-.371	-1.227	-1.812
	(.962)	(3.784)	(1.128)	(.254)	(1.129)	(1.149)
R-square	.12	.04	.25	.06	.08	.08
Wisconsin Democrats						
competitiveness	-.057	-.019	-.098	-.388	-.090	.009
	(.018)	(.022)	(.025)	(.188)	(.038)	(.023)
comp. squared	.002		.003	.008	.003	
	(.0004)		(.0005)	(.004)	(.0008)	
nonincumbent	-.079	-.452	.693	-.257	.643	.042
	(.173)	(.685)	(.225)	(1.672)	(.369)	(.878)
constant	.095	1.917	-.161	6.599	.096	.914
	(.220)	(.745)	(.298)	(2.212)	(.419)	(.904)
R-square	.57	.02	.53	.05	.36	.00
Wisconsin Republicans						
competitiveness	.050	.071	-.048	.019	-.039	.019
	(.014)	(.038)	(.047)	(.019)	(.037)	(.035)
comp. squared			.002		.002	
			(.0008)		(.0007)	
nonincumbent	.095	.460	.088	-.104	.619	-2.039
	(2.970)	(.825)	(.269)	(.387)	(.346)	(1.025)
constant	-.814	-1.852	.421	-.247	-.010	1.591
	(.604)	(1.675)	(.754)	(.655)	(.538)	(1.452)
R-square	.14	.04	.27	.01	.18	.08

Continued on next page

Table 6-1—*Continued*

	1982		1984		1986	
	LCC	LPACS	LCC	LPACS	LCC	LPACS
All Democratic Campaign Committees						
competitiveness	-.039	-.165	-.027	-.136	-.117	-.106
	(.034)	(.073)	(.013)	(.048)	(.022)	(.026)
comp. squared	.001	.004	.001	.003	.003	.003
	(.0006)	(.001)	(.0003)	(.001)	(.0004)	(.001)
nonincumbent	.465	.341	.557	.589	.689	.366
	(.216)	(.463)	(.111)	(.427)	(.190)	(.230)
constant	.177	1.569	.292	3.656	.242	.464
R-square	.13	.11	.18	.09	.19	.09
All Republican Campaign Committees						
competitiveness	-.050	.071	-.085	-.057	-.037	-.065
	(.047)	(.021)	(.032)	(.038)	(.023)	(.033)
comp. squared	.002		.003	.002	.002	.002
	(.0007)		(.0006)	(.0004)	(.0005)	(.0007)
nonincumbent	.910	1.122	.743	.745	.976	-.003
	(.184)	(.392)	(.261)	(.306)	(.203)	(.288)
constant	-.613	-2.295	.241	-.756	.327	.553
R-square	.18	.05	.09	.07	.11	.06

targeted their resources on close races to a higher degree than the Missouri Democrats' leadership PACs, but this difference was reversed for the Washington Democrats in 1982 whose leadership PACs were better at targeting competitive races.

The similarity in targeting marginal races between caucus campaign committees and leadership PACs holds up when all of the states are combined for a single analysis of Democratic and Republican committees. In 1984 and 1986, only marginal differences existed between the two types of committees for each party in terms of the relationship between the measures of competitiveness and the proportion of campaign committee funds that a candidate receives. In 1982, the Democratic leadership PACs appear to have been better than the caucus committees at concentrating their resources in close races.[4]

Support for the argument that caucus campaign committees and leadership PACs differ in the emphasis given to nonincumbent candidates—hypothesis 5—requires that the coefficients for the nonincumbency variable in table 6-1 be greater in a positive direction for caucus campaign committees than for leadership PACs. This is the case in twenty-two of the thirty-two sets of committees. 1982 had the most cases that did not fit the relationship. Because redistricting leads to greater uncertainty regarding reelection for incumbents, the poor showing in 1982 is likely the result of the redistricting that occurred in most states just prior to the 1982 elections. As reported in chapter 5, many of the caucus committees do give priority to incumbents in trouble, and in an election following a redrawing of the legislative districts the number of incumbents in trouble is likely to be much higher than in other years. By 1986 all but two caucus campaign committees gave a greater emphasis than leadership PACs to nonincumbents.

In Missouri, the opposite is found, that is, leadership campaign committees seem to be more likely than caucus campaign committees to fund nonincumbents, as indicated by the larger coefficient for nonincumbency. This finding is the result of two factors. One is the fact that the state is dominated by the Democrats. Under this condition, as demonstrated in chapter 5, caucus campaign committees will be more likely to fund incumbents to protect their majority and will have little incentive to support nonincumbents. The other is the youthful status of the these committees. Both parties' caucus campaign committees did not really come into existence until 1984, and both parties' caucus committees began as "incumbent trust funds"; that is, they collected funds from incumbents and returned those funds at election time if needed.

Why leadership PACs fund more nonincumbents under these conditions, however, is a mystery—it certainly does not conform to expectations. It may be that the emphasis placed on incumbents by caucus campaign committees creates a situation where leadership contributions can have more of an effect by funding nonincumbents. It may also be that leadership PACs in Missouri fund nonincumbents in order to enlarge the number of seats held by a faction within the Democratic legislative party. As plausible as the second argument seems, it is not the impression I received in my discussions with minority leader James Talent or with Mark Ausmus, the Speaker's General Counsel. Representative Talent indicated that his leadership PAC was "a question of me trying to help others who need it," and that it was "not used to affect leadership races." Ausmus indicated that legislators who want to contribute to other campaigns often do so after calling the speaker or himself for information regarding candidates who need help. Consequently, the greater willingness of leadership PACs to fund nonincumbents must result from a situation where incumbents receive sufficient enough attention from the caucus committees, leaving nonincumbents as the candidates which leadership PACs can help the most.

When the data from all of the states are merged, the tendency for caucus campaign committees to place a greater emphasis than leadership PACs on nonincumbent candidates is clearly evident in three out of the six cases—the Democratic committees in 1982 and 1986 and the Republican committees in 1986. Considering the fact that the co-efficient for leadership PACs fails to attain an acceptable level of significance for Democrats in 1984; it cannot be said that the coefficient significantly differs from zero, it may be said that in four out of the six cases caucus campaign committees are more likely to emphasize nonincumbent candidates than leadership PACs.

Reflecting the findings in the separate analyses of the committees, the 1982 results for the Democratic caucus campaign committees are only marginally greater than the results for the Democratic leadership PACs. The Republicans in 1982 represent the one case where the leadership PACs actually outdo the caucus committees in funding nonincumbent candidates. For both parties in 1982 this may be because of reapportionment. For the Republicans the findings may also be because 1982 was a poor year for Republicans in terms of party popularity, a condition that might have lead to a "defensive" strategy on the part of caucus committees, that is, one involving the protection of incumbents. Such a possibility will be more thoroughly tested in the following chapter.

Conclusion

In most cases the difference in resource allocation between legislative party caucus campaign committees and legislative leadership PACs comes in the emphasis these committees place on funding caucus outsiders. Both types of legislative party campaign committees appear to concentrate their resources on close or competitive races to the same degree. Caucus campaign committees, however, tend to place a greater emphasis on funding nonincumbents.

The reason for the difference in funding nonincumbents originates more from the slight differences in the goals held by those who make the decisions for these committees than from the differences in the nature of the committees. Individual legislators in control of their own campaign committees are more likely to fund incumbents because such a strategy better serves the goals of individual legislators. Caucuses are concerned with control of the legislature and thus caucus campaign committees will actively seek to gain or maintain a majority of seats, a goal that requires a greater willingness to fund nonincumbent candidates.

One important consideration regarding the differences in resource allocation between caucus campaign committees and leadership PACs is the fact that, as demonstrated in chapter 4, not all caucus committees are similarly structured. Some caucus campaign committees allow for a great deal of participation from the entire caucus, others are more similar to leadership PACs in that they are almost entirely run by the party's leadership. Such structural differences should lead to differences among caucus campaign committees in their willingness to fund nonincumbents, obscuring the differences between caucus campaign committees and leadership PACs. Another condition that might obscure the differences is the level of party competition in the state and in the districts. Where party competition is low, funding nonincumbent candidates is much less likely to result in positive outcomes. These two conditions point to a limitation of the analysis presented in this chapter—too few states. Though the number of states included in this analysis goes far beyond any other research into legislative party campaign committees, more states are needed to disentangle the many factors shaping the decisions of those in charge of legislative party caucus campaign committees and leadership campaign committees. Such a requirement will likely go unfulfilled until more states make their campaign finance records more accessible and more uniform.

The future of the relationship between the two types of legislative party campaign committees is not completely clear at this point. Early on in the development of these committees, legislative caucus campaign committees were very similar to leadership PACs; they functioned mainly to distribute campaign contributions. Today, caucus campaign committees are becoming more like party organizations, involved in providing traditional party services and candidate-centered services, recruiting candidates, and directing contributions from other sources. Meanwhile, leadership PACs still act only to transfer money from one party member to another. The development of caucus campaign committees and leadership PACs has thus diverged, one specializing in assisting candidates through services, the other specializing in transferring excess campaign funds. The difference in the assistance each type of committee provides nonincumbents also suggests that caucus committees and leadership PACs perform separate functions, one a party function, the other a career function for the individual legislator. These differences in caucus campaign committees and leadership PACs suggest that the reason for the existence of both types of committees continues to exist, making it likely that both will continue to operate, barring any state legislative action to prohibit or restrict such activity.

7
Strategic Variations in Caucus Campaign Committee Tactics

The previous chapters demonstrated that legislative party campaign committees strategically distribute their resources to both incumbent and nonincumbent candidates in close races. The purpose of this chapter is to explore the possibility that the strategies pursued by these campaign committees are more complex. Specifically, this chapter investigates the possibility that legislative party caucus campaign committees adjust their strategies according to their status within the legislature and according to trends in party popularity at the state and national level. Minority party campaign committees and campaign committees whose party is enjoying a surge in popularity at either the state or national level are expected to pursue an offensive strategy entailing an emphasis on nonincumbent candidates. Majority party campaign committees and campaign committees whose party is suffering in terms of popularity are expected to pursue a defensive strategy entailing an emphasis on protecting their party's incumbent legislators. The results of the analysis indicate that some but not all of the legislative party campaign committees appear to follow such strategies.

Majority v. Minority Party Status

An effective use of resources to attain the goal of majority party status may require more than a simple strategy of supporting candidates in competitive races. A minority party must actively recruit and support open seat candidates and challengers in order to increase the number of seats they hold in the legislature. This "offensive" strategy is the only way that they can attain majority status. Members of the legislative party caucus, according to the theoretical propositions developed and tested in the previous chapters are willing to forgo the contributions they would receive from the committee in order to attain the goal of majority party status. Members of a minority legislative party caucus campaign committee should be even more willing to do so, because the change from minority to majority status would mean a greater payoff (in terms of committee assignments and success of favored legislation). Thus, minority party legislative caucus campaign committees should exhibit a greater willingness to fund nonincumbent candidates. Once again, this calculus will be different for legislatures dominated by one party. When the chances of a change in the party's status are very small, the goal of majority party status is not a priority and the willingness to allow committee funds to go to outsiders does not exist.

All a majority legislative caucus campaign committee has to do to meet the goal of majority party status is to make sure that the party retains all of its legislative seats. In other words, the majority party must insure that its incumbents are reelected and that the party wins any open seats created by a retirement of one of their incumbents. Because incumbents are almost unbeatable at the national and state level, the most efficient way to distribute the committees' resources to attain the goal of majority status is to use the resources to reinforce the incumbency advantage.[1] Thus, majority party legislative caucus campaign committees should follow a defensive strategy that puts a top priority on defending vulnerable incumbents. Unlike the minority party committees, this strategy is likely to be more prevalent as the size of the majority increases.

These arguments lead to the hypothesis first presented in chapter 2:

> 6. Minority legislative caucus campaign committees that have a reasonable chance of winning a majority of seats should be found to concentrate a greater proportion of their resources on nonincumbent candidates than their majority party counterparts.

The Effects of Partisan Trends in Popularity

In attempting to gain or maintain a majority it might also be expected that the legislative caucus campaign committees would take advantage of swings in party popularity to increase the number of seats they hold. When the public's perception of the party is positive, for example, because of having a popular candidate at the top of the ticket, campaign committees may try to "cash in" on that popularity by supporting nonincumbent candidates and in that way increase their seats in the legislature. High popularity, it is assumed, will translate into votes. In this way a legislative party is using trends in partisan support among the public to counter the incumbency advantage.

If public perceptions of the party are negative, because of such things as a scandal or views that the party is not handling the job of governing well, campaign committees may try to counteract these trends to avoid losing what they already have. In other words, legislative caucus campaign committees whose state or national party's popularity is low should be found to focus their efforts on defending weak incumbents. In this way parties on the down end of a partisan trend make use of the incumbency advantage to try to reduce the effects of the negative changes in partisan support among the electorate.[2]

These arguments lead to the following hypotheses:

7. Legislative party caucus campaign committees whose party is enjoying a surge of popularity nationally should be more likely to fund nonincumbent candidates than legislative party caucus campaign committees of the opposition.
8. Legislative party caucus campaign committees whose party is enjoying a surge of popularity at the state level should be more likely to fund nonincumbent candidates than legislative party caucus campaign committees of the opposition.

Alternatively, it may be that the claim that "all politics is local" is true in the case of legislative caucus campaign committees.[3] That is, it is possible that decision makers focus mainly on district level forces—closeness of the previous race, strength of the candidates, and local politics—in their decisions, ignoring national or statewide trends.

Analysis

Testing these offensive/defensive hypotheses involves a further examination of the results of the regressions run in Chapter 6. The reader will recall that individual regressions were run for each party committee, regressing the proportion of the committee funds received by each candidate on the closeness of the race (the previous margin for 1984 and 1986, and the average margin for 1982), the square of the closeness measure, and incumbency status of the candidate (a dummy variable equaling 1 if the candidate was not an incumbent, and 0 if the candidate was an incumbent).[4] Or:

$$PROPLPCC = b_0 + b_1(COMPETITION) + b_2(COMPETITION)^2 + b_3NONINC + e$$

where PROPLPCC is the proportion of legislative party campaign committee total resources received by a candidate, COMPETITION is the measure of closeness, and NONINC is the dummy variable for incumbency status. The proportional dependent variable was used to make the results comparable across parties, committees and states.

Party Status.   If, as hypothesized, the status of the legislative party has an impact on the way the legislative party resources are distributed, minority legislative party caucus campaign committees that have a realistic chance of attaining a majority should be found to be more likely to fund nonincumbents than the majority parties. That is, the effect of incumbency status (in this case measured as nonincumbency) on the contributions received from caucus campaign committees should be greater for minority party caucus campaign committees. To determine whether or not this is indeed the case, the coefficient for the variable measuring incumbency status in model 7-1 are presented in table 7-1.[5] Minority party caucus campaign committees' results are in bold. Means of the nonincumbent coefficients for all states are presented at the bottom of the table to provide an overall comparison of minority and majority committees. Two sets of means are presented, one including all cases and the second excluding the three states that are the lowest in party competition—Tennessee, Missouri, and Indiana.

Focusing first on the means of the nonincumbent coefficients for all states, a comparison of majority and minority caucus campaign committee lends support for the hypothesized relationship between party status and the funding of nonincumbents in two of the three years. Minority party caucus campaign committees in 1984 and 1986 were slightly more likely than majority caucus campaign committees to allocate a greater proportion of their resources to nonincumbents candidates. When the caucus campaign committees of entrenched

Table 7-1. Effect of Party Status and Trends on Candidates
Supported*

	1982	1984	1986
California			
Democrats	NA	NA	2.307
Republicans	1.104**	3.152	1.907
Illinois			
Democrats	-.605	-.138	-.424
Republicans	.054	**NA**	.750
Indiana			
Democrats	.097	-1.005	1.172
Republicans	-.719	-.905	-.143
Minnesota			
Democrats	.505	.678	.208
Republicans	.390	.339	.557
Missouri			
Democrats	none	-.253	-.319
Republicans	none	-1.384	.331
New York			
Democrats	NA	.021	.109
Republicans	NA	.914	.294
Oregon			
Democrats	1.829	1.197	1.547
Republicans	2.190	1.675	2.913
Tennessee			
Democrats	-.468	.684	.953
Republicans	-1.733	-1.471	-.640
Washington			
Democrats	.131	1.172	1.024
Republicans	.707	1.872	1.159
Wisconsin			
Democrats	-.079	.693	.643
Republicans	.095	.088	.619
Majority Party Committees			
nonincumbent	.261	.350	.625
Minority Party Committees			
nonincumbent	.209	.464	.871
Minority Party Committees			
without Low Party Competition			
States			
nonincumbent	.551	1.340	1.012

*Nonincumbent coefficients obtained from regressing the proportion of caucus committee funds on incumbency status, the previous margin, and the square of the previous margin.
** The figures for party committees that were in the minority before the election are in bold.

minority parties are excluded from the calculation—because, as argued above, their limited chance of winning a majority would eliminate the reason for supporting caucus outsiders—the differences between majority and minority caucus campaign committees is much more distinct. With the minority party caucus campaign committees from states with a dominant party excluded, the nonincumbent coefficient means for minority parties is clearly larger than the mean for majority parties in every year.

The mean of the nonincumbent coefficients for the majority party caucus campaign committees in 1986 was .625 and the mean for minority parties was 1.012. On average, a nonincumbent candidate of a minority party was likely to receive 1.012 percent of a caucus committee's resources, while a nonincumbent candidate of a majority parties was likely to receive .625 percent of the caucus committee's total resources (controlling for the closeness of the race).

Care must be taken in drawing conclusions from these composite results because aggregate-level patterns may mask differences on an individual level. A state by state comparison of minority and majority campaign committee support for nonincumbents shows that the pattern of greater minority party emphasis on nonincumbents holds for twelve of the twenty-five pairs of caucus campaign committees.[6] But because Missouri, Indiana, and Tennessee were not expected to evidence this distinction (because of the low levels of interparty competition), it can be said that in ten out of seventeen cases the minority party was likely to give greater assistance to nonincumbent candidates than the majority party.

Thus, the analysis of the effect of legislative party status provides limited support for the hypothesis that party status affects how legislative party caucus campaign committees distribute their resources. It apparently affects how some committees allocate their resources, but it seems to have no effect on others. The fact that not all minority legislative caucus campaign committees provide greater assistance to nonincumbent candidates than the majority party committees may be caused by any number of factors. It may be because of the state's political culture, the behavior of other actors in the elections, or it may be that the hypothesis is invalid. One other possible explanation is that legislative caucus campaign committees also adjust their resource allocation strategy over time, according to partisan trends. It is to this possibility that the analysis now turns.

Partisan Trends.   To determine whether or not legislative party caucus campaign committees vary their distribution strategy according to national or state party trends, the coefficients in table 7-1 will be compared again, but this time in terms of which party benefited from favorable public opinion before the election. National partisan trends are assessed based upon presidential and congressional elections. The partisan trends were in favor of the Republicans in 1984, the year that Reagan won the presidency in a landslide. The trends favored the Democrats in 1982, the year in which the recession peaked, and in 1986, when the Democrats won back control of the Senate and gained seats in the house. State trends in partisan support are gauged by the results of gubernatorial and/or U.S. Senate races.

If the decision makers in the legislative caucus campaign committees take into account trends in party popularity in their distribution strategies two patterns should be found in the regression results. First, Democratic and Republican caucus campaign committees should be found to differ in distribution strategies with regard to nonincumbents in any one year. Second, caucus campaign committees' distribution strategies should be found to change over time with regard to support for nonincumbents. The difference in resource distribution should be such that the caucus campaign committees give a greater proportion of their funds to nonincumbents when party fortunes are high and a greater proportion to incumbents when party popularity is down. This should be reflected in table 7-1 in terms of the size of the coefficients for nonincumbents, with higher positive coefficients meaning that the caucus campaign committee placed a greater emphasis on nonincumbents in that election cycle. Table 7-1 is organized in such a way as to facilitate comparisons within each year (down) and within each caucus campaign committee across the three years (across).

If national party trends have any impact, one should expect to find that the Republicans would give a greater proportion of their funds to nonincumbents in 1984, the year Ronald Reagan won the presidency in a landslide victory over Walter Mondale, and Democrats should be found to give a greater proportion of their funds to nonincumbents in 1982 and 1986. Looking first at each individual year, there is evidence—in terms of the difference between the two party committees within each state—that some of the legislative party caucus committees follow national party trends. Comparing the nonincumbent coefficients in each state, the pattern holds for three out of seven states in 1982—Indiana, Minnesota, and Tennessee— four out of seven in 1984—Indiana, New York, Oregon, and Washington—and four out of seven in 1986—California, Indiana, Tennessee, and Wisconsin. In total, the pattern holds in less than half of the states. Of those states, Indiana seemed to be the most in tune with national party trends. In fact, the Indiana House Republicans were one of the few committees, according to Jeff Estich, the Republican speaker pro tempore, to considered the effects of national and state party trends when making caucus campaign committee decisions. In Indiana 1986 the Democrats gave on average 1.172 percent more of their resources to nonincumbents in close races while the Republicans figure was −.143 percent.

Considering each individual committee over time, only seven of the fifteen committees appear to be adjusting their strategy for changes in national partisan trends from year to year. The Indiana Democrats, one positive case, in 1982 and 1986, were more likely to give a greater proportion of their resources to nonincumbents, and in 1984 were more likely to allocate a greater proportion to incumbents. As expected, the pattern of resource allocation for the California Republicans was just the reverse—higher emphasis on nonincumbents in 1984. For Minnesota Democrats the pattern was the opposite of what was expected for Democrats nationally in 1984, which may have something to do with the fact that the Democratic presidential candidate was from Minnesota, which also was the only state he won.

The failure to find a consistent pattern in the data that would suggest that decision makers on caucus campaign committees take national trends into consideration in distributing their resources, may indicate that state party trends are more important, or that local, district-level factors are more important. An examination of statewide elections results in these states might provide insight into the effect of state party trends. The Indiana Republicans had a greater emphasis on incumbents in 1984, over 1982 and 1986—a pattern just the opposite of what would be expected if national party trends were followed. This may be due in part to the competitive race for the governor's seat between the incumbent Republican Robert Orr, who won only 52 percent of the vote, and his Democratic opponent, W. Townsend who won 47 percent in 1984. The distribution pattern evidenced by the New York Assembly Democrats can not be explained by either state or national party trends. This may be due to the mixed signals the voters were giving in 1986 by reelecting Democratic Governor Cuomo with a 65 percent margin, while reelecting Republican Senator Alfonse D'Amato by a 57 percent margin.

The Washington House Democratic Caucus Committee's increase in support for nonincumbents in 1984—another finding that goes against the grain of national trends—may be explained by state politics because a Democratic challenger unseated a Republican incumbent governor that year. The results in Minnesota can be explained by Mondale's candidacy in 1984. The pattern for the Illinois Democrats is one in which nonincumbents in each year are given less of an emphasis than incumbents: the values are negative for each year. Nonincumbents were a little more likely to receive help from the Illinois Democratic Majority Committee in 1984.[7] This reversal of what would be expected given national partisan trends, may be because of state level politics, namely, the strong candidacy of incumbent governor Jim Thompson in 1982 and 1986 and, in 1984, the candidacy of Paul Simon, who won the Illinois Senate seat from incumbent Charles Percy despite the landslide victory for Reagan.[8] The distribution of legislative caucus committee resources by Democrats in Oregon and both parties in Wisconsin cannot be explained by either national or state party trends. For Oregon, this may be because of the weakness of the political parties in Oregon.

Thus, information about national and state party trends allows us to explain the differences in resource distribution patterns among most of the caucus campaign committees. What can not be established from this data, however, is whether or not this is a strategy pursued consciously or the result of an indirect impact of these trends on the resource distribution. It is possible that these findings are because of the impact that party trends have on the viability of candidates, on how competitive the races become, and even on the pool of quality candidates. That is, it may be that the partisan trends have only an indirect effect on the distribution of resources.

To determine whether or not legislative party caucus campaign committees consciously factored national and state party trends into their strategies, legislators and staff members who were interviewed were asked whether this occurred. Responses were overwhelmingly negative, sometimes with the comment that legislative electoral politics is local politics (see appendix for questionnaire). A few exceptions were found. The Illinois House Republicans and the Democrats in both chambers indicated that both national and state trends were taken into consideration when their caucus campaign committee made its decisions.[9] Steve Brown, who works with the Illinois Democratic Majority Committee in the house, indicated that the IDMC does take national and state partisan trends into consideration, but that "the effect was qualified by local politics." Indiana House Republicans claimed to follow national and state party trends, and the Wisconsin Speaker admitted that they consider national party trends in their decisions, but only for the few legislative districts that are close to the major media markets of Chicago and Minneapolis/St. Paul.

The rest of the responses from representatives of caucus campaign committees indicated that national and state partisan trends were not considered. A few fell back on the maxim that "all politics is local," and others indicated that they are aggressive every year. An example of the tendency for partisan trends to be neglected was provided by Senator Charles Pray, president of the Maine Senate, who illustrated this with a description of the 1980 legislative races. In that year, according to Pray, there was "an exceptionally good crop of Democratic challengers." The Senate Democratic caucus campaign committee backed these candidates and, as a result, won seven seats and a majority in that year, the same year that Republicans took over the White House and the U.S. Senate. A number of committees admitted that they worked with the national or state candidates, as in having candidates make appearances with presidential candidates, but denied that they consciously adjusted strategy of funding candidates according to national or state party politics.

Thus, although the regression analysis displays some patterns that suggest a difference in strategy based upon party trends, state and national, interview responses indicate that, with few exceptions—mainly in Illinois—legislative party campaign committee decision makers do not consciously pursue such a strategy. Instead, according to the interview responses, it appears that local politics dominates decision making. The patterns that were found in the analysis, then, must be a result of an indirect effect that party trends have on the distribution of resources. That is, what must be happening is that partisan conditions shape the nature of the competition in legislative districts, determining which races will be close, which in turn affects the committees' distribution of resources. Generally speaking, there is no evidence that those who control legislative parties react consciously to partisan trends as the political elites in Jacobson and Kernell's research.[10]

Combined Effects of Party Status and Partisan Trends

The separate analyses of the effects of party status and partisan trends does not take into account that both of these factors are working on the distribution of resources at the same time. Consequently, to more accurately assess the effect of these influences on legislative caucus campaign committees' strategy a more sophisticated analysis is needed. The purpose of this section is to report results from a multiple regression analysis of the combined effects of party status and popularity on legislative caucus campaign committee strategy. To test for the independent effects of party status and party popularity the data for all of the states was combined into one data set for regression analysis. Since the interest here is essentially in the effect party status and partisan trends have on a nonincumbent's share of caucus committee resources, the most appropriate regression model is one that incorporates an interaction effect between incumbency status and these factors. The regression model, then, involves regressing the proportion of caucus campaign committee resources received by each candidate on: the interaction between a dummy variable for candidate's party's status and a dummy for incumbency status; the interaction between a dummy variable for the effect of state partisan trends and national partisan trends and incumbency status; and measures of the closeness of the race and dummy variables for each state as controls. Formally, the model is such that:

$$PROPLPCC = b_0 + b_1(COMPETITION) + b_2(COMPETITION)^2 +$$
$$b_3(NONINC) + b_4(NONINC * PARTYSTAT) + b_5(NONINC *$$
$$PARTY) + b_6(NONINC * STPARTYTR) + b_7(CALIFORNIA) \ldots$$
$$+ b_{14}(WASHINGTON) + e$$

where COMPETITION is the measure of the closeness of the race, NONINC is the dummy variable for incumbency status (equaling 1 if the candidate is a nonincumbent and 0 if otherwise), PARTYSTAT is the dummy variable for party status (equaling 1 if the candidate's party is the minority party, 0 if otherwise), PARTY is the dummy variable for party (equalling 1 for Democrats and 0 for Republicans; this variable is used to assess national partisan trends), STPARTYTR is the dummy variable for state partisan trends (equaling 1 if the trend was in favor of the candidate's party, 0 if otherwise),[11] and CALIFORNIA through WASHINGTON are dummy variables for each state, excluding one from the analysis.[12] Setting up the model this way allows for the combination of what is essentially two different equations for each hypothesized relationship into one equation.[13]

Table 7-2 presents the results for this regression for each of the years of the analysis. As in all previous analyses the relationship between the contributions and the competitiveness of the race is positive, and significant, providing yet one more confirmation of the fact that legislative caucus campaign committees strategically concentrate their resources in close races.

Turning to the hypothesized differences in strategies, the coefficients of the interaction terms provide an indication of whether or not minority parties are more likely than majority party committees to provide greater support to nonincumbents.[14] In the model estimated for 1984, the coefficient for the interaction of party status and nonincumbency does provide support for the hypothesized relationship

Table 7-2. Combined Effects of Party Status and Party Popularity*

Variables	1982	1984	1986
competition	.054**	-.063**	-.075**
competition squared		.002**	.002**
nonincumbent	.024	.251**	.514**
noninc * minority status	.193	.474**	.105
noninc * state party trend	.378**	.413**	.135
noninc * national party trend	-.093	-.109	.019
Wisconsin	.031	.053	.060
California	.534**	.280	.455**
Oregon	.586**	-.488**	.316
Illinois	.380**	.143	-.066
Indiana	---	-.340	-.354
Tennessee	1.552**	.717**	.770**
Washington	-.108	-.431**	-.345
Missouri	---	.091	.197
Minnesota	-.219	-.576**	-.600**
(Constant)	-.1067**	.376**	-.188
R-square	.14	.12	.16

*Unstandardized regression coefficients obtained from regressing the proportion of caucus campaign committee contributions on the variables.
** Significant at the .05 level or better.

between party status and a caucus campaign committee's support for nonincumbents—it is significant and in the right direction. Nonincumbents of minority parties were likely to receive almost three times more of their caucus campaign committee funds than nonincumbents of majority parties. Nonincumbents of a minority party received .725 percent (.251 + .474) of their party's caucus committees resources while nonincumbents of majority parties were likely to receive .251 percent of their party's caucus committee funds. Thus, in 1984 minority parties put a greater emphasis on funding nonincumbent candidates than did majority parties (controlling for the effects of party trends). Though the coefficients are in the expected direction for 1982 and 1986, their failure to attain a satisfactory level of significance means that these results cannot be said to indicate that minority parties place a greater emphasis on nonincumbents than majority parties in these elections.

Evidence that state party trends increase caucus campaign committees' willingness to fund caucus outsiders is found in 1982 and 1984. Nonincumbents of parties that had a good year in 1982 were likely to receive .378 percent of their caucus committee funds (.378 + 0, 0 because the nonincumbent coefficient is not statistically significantly different from 0), while the proportion received by nonincumbents of parties that were not having a good year was 0. The lack of support for nonincumbents in 1982 is consistent with the findings in the previous chapter, and is undoubtedly because of the effect that reapportionment has on the security of incumbent candidates. Following the redrawing of legislative districts the electoral security of incumbents is probably at its lowest, leading caucus campaign committees to invest heavily in incumbents in the election year following redistricting. In 1984, nonincumbents of parties that were enjoying a good year at the state level were likely to receive .664 percent (.413 + .251) of their caucus committee funds, while nonincumbents of other state parties received .251 percent. Note that the coefficient for the nonincumbent variable is still significant and positive in 1984 and 1986, lending additional support to the hypothesized emphasis caucus campaign committees place on nonincumbents.

Thus, after combining all of the caucus campaign committee data, evidence of varying distribution strategies is not very strong. Minority parties were more likely to fund nonincumbent candidates than majority party committees but only in 1984. Positive state partisan trends also increased the proportion of caucus campaign committee funds received by a caucus outsider in 1982 and 1984. No impact of national party trends is evident in any year—a finding which, given the responses from legislative leaders and caucus campaign staff, is not very surprising.

Conclusion

While there seems to be evidence that some legislative caucus campaign committees in certain years vary their strategies according to their status in the legislature and according to state or national party trends, generalized conclusions regarding all legislative caucus campaign committees would be erroneous given the results of this analysis. While differences do appear to exist between some minority and majority legislative caucus campaign committees, only in 1984 is there clear evidence that this can be generalized to all committees once other factors are controlled for. And while some caucus campaign committees evidence a pattern that suggests that they are considering the impact of national and state party trends on legislative election outcomes, the aggregate analysis indicates an effect only for state partisan trends after other factors are controlled for. Furthermore, the interview responses regarding this strategy indicate that, with few exceptions, any pattern that does exist is not the result of a conscious consideration of the impact of partisan trends.

8
Conclusion

The results of the research and analysis conducted for this book have lead to a large number of conclusions about legislative party campaign committees. Two conclusions—one regarding the impact that legislative party campaign committees have on the distribution of resources in legislative elections and the other the status of legislative caucus campaign committees—are by far the most important and thus deserve special attention.

The analysis of campaign contributions and the interview results made it very apparent that legislative party caucus campaign committees and leadership PACs are having a profound impact on the distribution of resources in legislative races. They represent a new source of campaign resources for candidates and their behavior results in the redistribution of old resources. Though the dollar value of the resources distributed by legislative party campaign committees represents a small proportion of all of the campaign money that is transferred in legislative elections, both types of committees were found to concentrate those resources in such a way as to maximize their effect. Legislative party campaign committees were found to target their resources, concentrating them in competitive races where they were needed the most. This distribution pattern included the provision of assistance to nonincumbents—a tactic that helps legislative parties build and maintain a majority. These findings were corroborated repeatedly by qualitative interview data and by subsequent analyses that focused on the proportion of caucus committee resources that went to candidates.

The role played by caucus campaign committees in providing new resources to campaigns was determined to be greater than what records of their expenditures would indicate because these committees also provide a number of important services to candidates. Services such as polling, media consultation and facilities, and mass mailings can be purchased by caucus campaign committees at volume discounts and passed on to candidates as in-kind contributions at much lower costs than if the candidates purchased the services themselves. Moreover, the difficulty of assigning value to many of these services will mean that they will most likely be undervalued when they are reported as contributions. Both of these practices stretch the influence of caucus campaign committees far beyond what their expenditures would indicate.

In addition to representing a new source of campaign assistance, the distribution of legislative party campaign committees' resources tends to have a redistributive effect on traditional resources in state legislative campaigns. Because typical contributors—individuals and PACs—want access to policy makers, they tend to contribute to the campaigns of those who will likely be members of the legislature— incumbents. An even better investment for such contributors is to give to legislative leaders—speakers, majority and minority leaders, whips, and chairs of important committees. This behavior results in a situation in which those who do not need any more money continue to receive it, and those who do need it are largely ignored. The development of leadership PACs and caucus campaign committees probably arose from this top-heavy distribution when leaders discovered that using their excess campaign funds to assist other candidates would help them attain other goals, goals unrelated to their own reelection. Consequently, leadership PACs and caucus campaign committees redistribute campaign contributions from incumbents in little need of the money to candidates in close races in great need of the money. This, according to the analysis, included nonincumbent candidates, who otherwise have a difficult time convincing contributors that they are a good investment. Moreover, caucus campaign committees were found to have a hand in directing the flow of cash from other contributors in legislative races—PACs and individuals— greatly enhancing their effect on the flow of campaign resources in state legislative elections.

The empirical analysis and interview results also made it very apparent that legislative party caucus campaign committees have developed, or are developing, into what are indisputably party organizations. As mentioned above, in addition to dispensing cash contributions, the caucus campaign committees provide many services geared toward the candidate-centered campaigns of today. Furthermore, a number of committees also provide candidate-nonspecific, or party, services such as registration and get-out-the-vote drives, computerized voter lists, and development of grass-roots organizations. Legislative party caucus campaign committees also seem to have some input into the selection of their party's nominees: almost all of the caucus campaign committees were involved in recruiting candidates and some involved themselves in primary battles. Caucus campaign committees influenced the ability of candidates to raise revenues from other sources, either directly, by soliciting PAC money, or indirectly, by giving a candidate a mark of legitimacy that assures contributors that the candidate is a good investment. Legislative caucus campaign committees also appear to be broad-based organizations, drawing their resources from a diverse set of sources, including individuals, all types of PACs, corporations, legislators, and national and state party organizations.

In terms of resource utilization, legislative party caucus committees were found to strategically allocate their resources in such a way as to differentiate them from those of nonparty contributors and to maximize their impact on elections, the party's status in the legislature, and legislative behavior. Legislative party campaign committees were found to target close races and to fund nonincumbents. In a number of instances the relative level of resources being provided to nonincumbents by minority party caucus campaign committees seemed to indicate that caucus campaign committee strategies are designed to maximize the effect the committees have on the balance of power within the legislature. Also, some caucus campaign committees in some states seemed to vary their allocation strategy to take advantage of partisan trends, though when asked about it, only a few contacts in the committees indicated that this was done consciously. These distributional patterns indicate that caucus campaign committees are operating for the purpose of building or maintaining the party's legislative majority—an inference that is overwhelmingly supported by the interview responses. This purpose differs from nonparty contributors, who give largely for the purpose of gaining access to, or influence over lawmakers.

Not all legislative party caucus campaign committees studied here have attained a level of organizational sophistication that would justify labeling them party organizations. The level of institutionalization and the degree to which caucus campaign committees approximate party organizations, clearly differs from state to state, and

sometimes within each state. The differences are in part because of
the maturity of the caucus campaign committees; the older committees are more sophisticated and more like party organizations. The diverse nature of the sample of states used in this research—states with
well established caucus committees that have existed for a decade or
more such as Wisconsin, Illinois, California and Minnesota; states
with newly formed caucus committees that are just beginning to develop such as Maine and Missouri; and one state, Indiana, with committees that have existed for a while and are just beginning to provide
more sophisticated services to candidates—allowed for comparisons
that provide support for the argument that time plays a major role in
the level of development of caucus campaign committees. But why
did caucus campaign committees appear earlier in some states than
others? The reason can be found in the explanations for why legislative parties became involved in elections in the first place—the increase in the cost of campaigns, the lack of assistance from other
regular party organizations, and the level of interparty competition.
The states with the oldest legislative party campaign committees, Illinois, New York, and California, have the most expensive campaigns
and are competitive states. The fact that the development of Democratic caucus campaign committees exceeded that of the Republicans
in a number of states—Wisconsin, Maine, and California—is a reflection of the relative organizational strength of Democratic and Republican state party organizations; because of better state organizations,
the need for Republican caucus campaign committees was not as
great. And the lack of serious competition in southern states explains
why caucus campaign committees have yet to develop in southern
legislative parties, though an effective legislative party organization
may be just what southern Republicans need to bring their party up
to a more competitive level.

Implications

Given the findings of this research, it should be clear that legislative
party campaign committees represent an important new development
with major implications for political parties, legislative behavior and
legislative elections. The existence of legislative caucus campaign
committees that can be considered party organizations indicates that
political scientists need to reassess the way state political parties, and
political parties in general, are perceived in terms of organization,

roles, and strength. Because legislative party campaign committees have an effect on the distribution of resources in legislative elections, their activity has implications for legislative elections and party competition in those elections, as well as implications for the public policy-making process at the state level.

The fact that legislative party caucus committees exist and resemble party organizations means that our understanding of the structure of state party organizations must change. The addition of legislative party organizations to the party structure at the state level means that many of the state parties now have the same specialized divisions that the national parties have, that is, legislative organizations that operate separately from the central party committees.

Furthermore, our understanding of the structure and functions of political parties in the U.S. in general needs some rethinking. Sorauf's classic conceptualization of political parties drew distinctions between the party organization, the party-in-government, and the party-in-the-electorate. This research, combined with the findings at the national level,[1] demonstrates that the lines between the party organization and the party-in-government may no longer be as clear as they once were. Congressional and state legislative parties have, in addition to their function of governing, entered into the business previously thought to be the sole realm of party organizations—political campaigns.

The development of legislative party campaign committees at the state level also says something about the viability of political parties in American politics. Until the mid- to late 1980s, a strong consensus existed among political scientists that the political parties were in a state of decline.[2] Piece by piece, new research on political parties has come to challenge this conclusion.[3] Political parties, some political scientists argue, are not continuing their decline, instead they have been adapting to the new age of candidate-centered campaigns. This adjustment is apparent in the types of services parties provide to candidates' campaigns and in the role parties are playing as brokers for resources valuable to campaigns. Before the research presented in this book, much of the evidence for this change in the political parties came from the national level.[4] The findings of this research show that this process of adaptation has spread to the state level, at least where legislative parties are concerned.

Legislative party campaign committee behavior also has major implications for legislative elections. The campaign committees are providing a new source of campaign resources in legislative elections and having a redistributive effect on the old sources. They collect resources from campaign contributors that would normally go to safe incumbents and redistribute them to candidates in close races. Legislators who feel they are safe, electorally, are also distributing their personal funds to candidates in close races. With national party organizations following the same strategy, the nature of competition in legislative elections is becoming one where the battle between the parties is focused on a handful of seats. These races attract all of the resources and attention, while the others—those involving incumbents—remain largely uncontested. Such a pattern reinforces the high rates of incumbency success and has normative implications for the level of accountability legislators are held to by their constituents. Add to this the effect of the politics of redistricting and even greater reinforcement is given to this pattern of competition in legislative elections.

On the other hand, it may also be argued that the resulting distribution of campaign resources increases competition. By shifting campaign resources from candidates in uncompetitive races to those in competitive races legislative party campaign committees are elevating the level of competition in those races. Their willingness to fund nonincumbents means that legislative party campaign committee activity may weaken the effect of incumbency and increase the responsiveness of legislators. An incumbent who knows that she could be targeted by the opposition's campaign committees may be more conscious of the demands of her constituents. There is, however, no evidence to date of any weakening of the incumbency advantage at the state level.

Because legislative party campaign committee financing of elections is done in an attempt to gain or maintain a majority of seats, legislative party campaign committee activity also should increase interparty competition in the states. Legislative caucus campaign committees represent a centralized organization committed to helping the candidates based on partisanship and thus furthering the interest of the party. These organizations, therefore, can only increase competition between the parties. Furthermore, minority parties' greater willingness to fund nonincumbents (a finding that, though evident in some states, was not universal) increases competition in races with incumbents, and increases the chance that they may gain a majority of seats. And, finally, legislative party campaign committee activity may expand the number of truly competitive seats if the resources they make available, and the candidates they recruit, have the effect of changing a district from marginally competitive to competitive.

The problem with assessing the effect of legislative party campaign committee activity on elections is similar to the problem associated with assessing the impact of money in general on elections—the effect of expectations on contributions. In other words, are candidates who spend more money more likely to win, or do candidates who are more likely to win attract more contributions? In the case of legislative party campaign committees' effect, it is a matter of whether legislative party campaign committees merely reinforce prior expectations regarding competitiveness, or whether the contributions they give make races more competitive. It is probably a combination of the two. The findings of this study indicate that prior expectations—as measured by the previous margin—are associated with the level of contributions, but the resources legislative campaign committees put into a race (sometimes as high as 60 percent of a candidate's total revenues) surely must have some impact. Whatever one may believe, this is clearly an interesting topic for future research on legislative party campaign committees.

The role that legislative party campaign committees play in legislative elections is likely to affect the policy-making process within the legislature. One of the important functions that political parties play in our political system is to bridge the gap created by the separation of powers at both the state and national level. The development of legislative party campaign committees may destroy a party's ability to provide this bridge if the committees' activities result in a more independent legislative party. Following reforms aimed at improving professionalism, legislatures have become much more independent of the governor. Having their own party organization, their own resources to win elections and communicate with the public, may increase this independence even more, making it hard for governors to have their way with legislatures. However, if cooperation between the legislative organization, the state party, and the governor's organization develops, legislative party campaign committees could lead to better relationships between the governor and legislators as equals in state government. This integration of the legislative party campaign committees can occur in a number of ways such as transfers from one organization to another, the sharing of poll information, or the merging of resources for phone banks or advertising. This research presented some evidence that such cooperation occurs. The financial records in a number of states such as California and Illinois show that caucus committees do indeed receive contributions from other campaigns, such as gubernatorial campaigns. And many of those interviewed indicated that there was cooperation with other party and candidate organizations.

The development of legislative party caucus and leadership campaign committees may also strengthen party ties by building party cohesion within the legislature. Given the way that legislative caucus campaign committees distribute their resources and the responses to the survey, the potential for increasing cohesion is quite real. Candidates in close races receive substantial contributions, cash and in-kind, from the legislative party campaign committees. This has the potential of making cohorts of legislators who are grateful to either the party caucus or to individual leaders. Such gratitude may result in greater party cohesion. Greater party unity may also develop if the campaign committees create an atmosphere that makes the caucus pull together as a team, united behind a common purpose. This was reported to have occurred among the Assembly Democrats in Wisconsin. It is clear from the interviews, however, that there is no attempt to increase party cohesion by distributing resources on the basis of party loyalty or ideology.

Because legislative party campaign committee activity represents a possible strengthening of the political parties, their development may also represent a better functioning of the role of political parties as a link between the people and government. By collecting resources from PACs and from legislators who received contributions from PACs, legislative party caucus campaign committees are placing an extra step or two between candidates and interest group influence. Such a development, along with the potential for greater party cohesion, means the parties may be moving, however slightly, toward the model of responsible parties: collective party goals are strengthened at the expense of the various special interests, allowing voters to more directly select policy alternatives through the selection of party candidates.

The other side of this development, however, is the possibility that by having legislative party caucus campaign committees collect interest group money, they may actually be centralizing interest group influence, consequently making it easier for interest groups to influence the policy-making process. This potential for centralized influence is illustrated by the Washington Senate Republicans who have developed a major donor program that gives financially powerful groups and individuals frequent and easy access to legislators (though it should be noted that Senate Minority Leader Hayner stated that one of the purposes of their caucus campaign committee was to "get people [legislators] interested in representing the public interest as opposed to special interests"). The fact that legislative party caucus committees draw their resources from a diverse set of contributors, however, means that the possibility of centralized influence by one interest is minimized. The problem this creates for policy representation, however, remains, because not all interests in society are organized or have the resources to contribute to legislative party campaign committees.

It appears that the campaign activities of legislative party campaign committees, one way or the other, will have an effect on policy representation either by increasing special interest representation or by increasing representation of the public. It is left to future research to determine how legislative party campaign committee activity influences policy representation.

The cynical view of the caucus campaign committees (that legislative party campaign committees become captives of the interests who provide the resources) is apparently the basis for attacks on these committees by "good government" groups in California and New York. In California Proposition 73 has temporarily ended legislative party campaign committee activity. In New York, the campaign committees were recently the target of investigations by the New York Commission on Governmental Integrity. During the hearings held by the commission, Speaker Miller defended the campaign committees declaring that in raising the money for the committees "there are no promises to be made, there are no quid pro quos to be made, there is no pressure to be bought."

Whether or not this backlash spreads to other states remains to be seen. It may depend upon party politics and upon which form of organization is attacked. Leadership PACs' similarity to PACs in general may make them easier targets, especially if they have been used for political in-fighting within the legislature.

California represents a case where partisan politics was involved. The Republicans, who relied much less on their caucus campaign committees and leadership PACs than on their state party, campaigned in favor of the proposition that would ban legislative party campaign committees while the Democrats, whose legislative party campaign committees gave them an advantage in legislative elections, campaigned against it. The result—passage of Proposition 73—was to hand the Democrats a significant setback in their attempt to play a role in legislative elections. Where such a difference exists between the parties in other states, good government groups may find an ally in the party that relies less on legislative party campaign committees—most likely Republicans because of their stronger state party organizations—and use this alliance to achieve a ban on caucus campaign committees or leadership PACs, or limits on such practices. Given the conclusion that legislative caucus campaign committees are party organizations, the implication is that attempts to destroy these organizations represent one party attempting to gain or maintain an advantage by leveling its attack at the other party's new form of organization. An organization that is different from state party organizations only in its location (within the legislature) and in the fact that it has not attained a level of acceptance among the public.

Appendix

Leadership Interview Schedule

Name _____ Date: _____ / __ /89
State _____ Phone: (_____) _____
Position _____
Committee Name _____
Chamber: __ Senate __ House
Party: __ Democrat __ Republican

I. *Legislative Caucus Campaign Committees*: I would like to ask you a number of questions about the operation of your party's legislative caucus campaign committee.

A. *Structure*: First I would like to ask you a few questions about how the caucus campaign committee works.

1. Does the caucus have an actual campaign committee that makes the decisions?

2. How many legislators are involved in the operation of the committee?

3. How are they selected for the committee?
   __ elected by caucus members
   __ selected by the leadership
   __ other _____

4. How much control or influence would you say the leadership (the speaker, the minority leader, or the majority leader) has over the committee decisions?

5. How much control or influence would you say the state party organization has over the committee's decisions?

6. Is there a staff? __ yes __ no

B. *Campaign Support Provided*

1. What types of campaign assistance does your party's caucus campaign committee provide candidates?
   __ money
   __ services
   If in-kind services, what types?
   __ polling
   __ campaign consultants
   __ mailing lists
   __ advertisement
   __ campaign seminars

___ fund raising help
___ lists of contributors
___ other _____

2. Does the committee play any role in the recruitment of candidates? If so, is the availability of assistance from the committee used as an inducement?

C. *Distribution Decisions*: Now I would like to ask you a few questions about the caucus campaign committee's decisions regarding the distribution of campaign funds.

1. What are the criteria used in order to decide how to distribute the campaign resources? How does the committee decide who to assist? Do they have to meet any particular standards? If yes, what are they?

2. Are any adjustments made over the course of the election season? If so, what type of information are they based upon?

3. Does the committee tend to give any preference to incumbents over nonincumbents or the other way around?

4. In making its decisions in terms of which candidates to assist, incumbents versus challengers, does the committee give any consideration to national or state party trends?

5. Does the committee provide assistance for candidates in primary contests?

D. *Goals*:

1. What is the committee trying to accomplish in funding legislative races? What are your reasons for collecting money and providing assistance? Are there any other reasons?

2. How effective has it been effective in meeting those goals?

E. *Impact*:

1. What type of effect do you feel the committees assistance has on the outcome of elections?

2. Does the fact that your committee provides assistance to a candidate help those candidates raise funds from other sources, e.g., PACs?

3. Does this activity have any impact on the behavior of legislators within the legislature?

F. *History*: I would like to ask you a little about the history of the committee.

1. To the best of your knowledge, how many years has the caucus campaign committee been involved in campaign finance? (how early)

2. Are you aware of any changes that have taken place in the purpose of the organization since it was first established, or in the criteria used in deciding which candidates to support.

G. *State Campaign Finance Laws*: How do campaign election laws affect how you decide to distribute the funds? Are there limits on expenditures?

H. *Source of Funds*: Where do the funds come from to supply this effort, what type of organizations?(rank)

___ individuals
___ business PACs

___ labor PACs
___ professional PACs
___ legislators
___ party organization
___ national party organization
___ local party organizations

I. Anything else that I should know about your caucus campaign committee?

II. *Leadership PACs*: In some states individual legislators, especially the leaders, have been found to distribute some of their own campaign funds to other legislative candidates,

A. Does this occur in your state?   ___ yes   ___ no

B. Do you participate?   ___ yes   ___ no

C. Any coordination with party caucus committees or state party organization?

    ___ caucus campaign committees
    ___ state party organization

D. Purpose of contributing funds?

E. Recipients of funds?

    ___ incumbents
    ___ challengers
    ___ open seat candidates

Notes

Introduction

1. Paul S. Herrnson, "Do Parties Make a Difference? The Role of Party Organizations in Congressional Elections," *Journal of Politics* 48 (1986); Herrnson, *Party Campaigning in the 1980s* (Cambridge, Mass.: Harvard Univ. Press); Gary C. Jacobson, "Party Organization and Distribution of Campaign Resources: Republicans and Democrats in 1982," *Political Science Quarterly* 4 (1985); Gary C. Jacobson, "Parties and PACs in Congressional Elections," in *Washington Reconsidered*, ed. Lawrence Dodd and Bruce Oppenheimer (Washington: Congressional Quarterly Press, 1985); David Adamany, "Political Parties in the 1980s," in *Money and Politics in the United States: Financing Elections in the 1980s*, ed. Michael Malbin (Chatham, N.J.: Chatham House, 1984).

2. Adamany, "Political Parties in the 1980s," 76-78.

3. See Herrnson, *Party Campaigning in the 1980s*.

4. Herrnson, *Party Campaigning in the 1980s*.

5. Malcolm Jewell and David Olson, *Political Parties and Elections in American States*, 3d ed. (Chicago: Dorsey, 1988). For examples of single state studies see Richard Clucas, "Campaign Suport as a Leadership Resource: A Case Study of Two California Assembly Speakers," paper presented at the 1989 Annual Meeting of the American Political Science Association; California Commission on Campaign Financing, *The New Gold Rush: Financing California Legislative Campaigns* (Los Angeles: Center for Responsive Government, 1985); Richard R. Johnson, "Partisan Legislative Campaign Committees: New Power, New Problems," *Illinois Issues* (July 1987); Mark Rom and Andre Aoki, "How Big the Pig: Wisconsin Campaign Contributions, Legislative Vote Scores, and the Party in Government," paper delivered at the 1987 Annual Meeting of the Northeast Political Science Association; Gary Rose, "Party Organization Activity in the 1986 Connecticut State Legislative Elections," paper delivered at the 1987 Annual Meeting of the Northeast Political Science Association; Jeffrey Stonecash, "Working at the Margins: Campaign Finance and Party Strategy in the New York Assembly Elections," *Legislative Studies Quarterly* 13 (1989).

1. Legislative Elections and Political Parties

1. See Gary C. Jacobson, *Money in Congressional Elections* (New Haven: Yale Univ. Press, 1980); and William P. Welch, "The Allocation of Political

Moneys: Parties, Ideological Groups, and Economic Interest Groups," working paper no. 72, Department of Economics, Univ. of Pittsburgh, 1977.

2. The full title of the study is "State Legislative Election Returns in the United States: 1968-1986," ICPSR study no. 8907.

3. See Jewell and Olsen, *Political Parties and Elections in American States*; Malcolm Jewell and David Breaux, "The Effect of Incumbency on State Legislative Elections," *Legislative Studies Quarterly* 13 (1989): 495-514.

4. See Malcolm Jewell, "The State of U.S. State Legislative Research," *Legislative Studies Quarterly* 6 (1981); and Richard Neimi and Laura Winsky, "Membership Turnover in State Legislatures: Trends and Effects of Districting," *Legislative Studies Quarterly* 12 (1987): 115-24.

5. See William Boyd, "Campaign Finance and Electoral Outcomes in Wisconsin and Georgia House Races," paper delivered at the 1982 Annual Meeting of the Midwest Political Science Association; David Breaux and Anthony Gierzynski, "Money in State Legislative Elections," paper delivered at the Lexington Conference on State Legislative Elections, Mar. 1990; Anthony Gierzynski and David Breaux, "Money and Votes in State House Elections," *Legislative Studies Quarterly* 16 (1991); Gregory Caldeira and Samuel Patterson, "Bringing Home the Votes: Electoral Outcomes in State Legislative Races," *Political Behavior* 4 (1982); Michael Giles and Anita Prichard, "Campaign Expenditures and Legislative Elections in Florida," *Legislative Studies Quarterly* 10 (1985): 71-88; Ruth S. Jones, "Financing State Elections," in *Money and Politics in the United State* (Chatham, N.J.: Chatham House, 1984), ed. Michael Malbin; John Owen and Edward Olson, "Campaign Spending and the Electoral Process in California, 1966-1974," *Western Political Quarterly* (1976); and William P. Welch, "The Effectiveness of Expenditures in State Legislative Races," *American Politics Quarterly* 4 (1976): 340-43.

6. See Caldeira and Patterson, "Bringing Home the Votes," and Giles and Pritchard, "Campaign Expenditures and Legislative Elections in Florida."

7. Leon Epstein, *Political Parties in the American Mold* (Madison, Wisc.: Univ. of Wisconsin Press, 1986); Frank Sorauf and Paul Allen Beck, *Party Politics in America*, 6th ed. (Glenview, Ill.: Scott, Foresman, 1988).

8. See Dean Walter Burnham, *The Current Crisis in American Politics* (New York: Oxford Univ. Press, 1982); David S. Broder, *The Party's Over: The Failure of Politics in America* (New York: Harper and Row, 1972); Austin Ranney, *Curing the Mischiefs of Faction: Party Reform in America* (Berkeley: Univ. of California Press, 1975); and William J. Crotty, *American Politics in Decline* (Boston: Little, Brown, 1984).

9. See Cornelius Cotter, James Gibson, John Bibby, and Robert Huckshorn, *Party Organization in American Politics* (New York: Praeger, 1984); Xandra Kayden, "The Nationalization of the Party System," in *Parties, Interest Groups and Campaign Finance Laws* (Washington: American Enterprise Institute, 1980), ed. Michael Malbin; Joseph A. Schlesinger, "The New American Political Party," *American Political Science Review* 79 (1985): 1151-69.

10. For additional evidence of the increasing cost of legislative campaigns, see Jewell and Olson, *Political Parties and Elections in the American States*, 155; Jones, "Financing State Elections," 175; and Sorauf, *Money in American Elections*, 156, 264.

11. Whether or not such increases in campaign expenditures should be measured in terms of constant dollars is debatable. Clearly it was much easier for a contributor to part with a larger sum of money in 1986 than it was in 1978 because of inflation. On the other hand, increases in the cost of campaigns, regardless of inflation, still represent pressure on candidates to raise more money from more sources than before.

12. It could be argued that the cause of the growth of the cost of legislative campaigns came from the growth in the availability of money and not because of the cost of new campaign technologies. This is a "chicken or egg" debate that is not important to the main thesis that legislative party caucus committees and leadership PACs emerged in the environment of costly legislative campaigns.

13. Jacobson, *Money in Congressional Elections*, and Welch, "The Allocation of Political Moneys."

14. See Paul Kleppner, *Who Voted? The Dynamics of Electoral Turnout, 1870–1980* (New York: Praeger, 1982); and Norman Nie, Sidney Verba, and John Petrocik, *The Changing American Voter* (Cambridge, Mass.: Harvard Univ. Press, 1979).

15. Richard F. Fenno, *Homestyle: House Members in Their Districts* (Boston: Little, Brown, 1978), found that U.S. Representatives are always insecure about reelection.

16. This argument is made by Schlesinger in "The New American Party."

17. If the difference in party control is considered, the change is even greater because two regions, the Northeast and the Midwest, witnessed a reversal of the majority party.

18. See Jacobson, *Money in Congressional Elections*; and Welch, "The Effectiveness of Expenditures in State Legislative Elections."

19. The data in table 1-2 invite a PROBIT analysis of the factors related to the existence of legislative party campaign committees in the fifty states, and in fact one was conducted. It was unsuccessful, however, because one of the most important determinants of the existence of the committees—the cost of legislative campaigns—is unavailable for all states. In the PROBIT analysis, the percentage difference in the seats held by the parties in the state and a measure of party organizational strength (borrowed from Cotter et al., *Party Organizations in American Politics* 1984) were used as indicators in the model.

20. See Cotter et al., *Party Organizations in American Politics*.

21. For a discussion of legislators' goals see Fenno, *Homestyle: Congressmen House Members in Their Districts*.

2. Theory and Method

1. See Robert Biersack and Clyde Wilcox, "The Role of Campaign Finance in Electoral Processes," paper presented at the 1989 Annual Meeting of the Midwest Political Science Association.

2. William P. Welch, "The Economics of Campaign Funds," *Public Choice* 20 (1974).

3. Welch, "The Economics of Campaign Funds." Also see Welch, "Allocation of Political Monies."

4. Herrnson, "Party Strategies and Resource Distribution in the 1984 Congressional Elections," manuscript.

5. In fact, efforts to combine rational choice and institutional approaches have been encouraged as of late; see James March and Johan Olson, "The New Institutionalism: Organizational Factors in Political Life," *American Political Science Review* 78 (1984); and Melissa Collie, "The Legislature and Distributive Policy Making in Formal Perspective," *Legislative Studies Quarterly* 13 (1988).

6. This argument is different from the ones made by the famous critics of the rational model, Herbert Simon and Charles Lindblom. Simon's and Lindblom's critiques also stress the limits of the individual in rational decision-making. Since this research focuses on political elites, the constraints arising from individual limitations are minimized.

7. Charles E. Lindblom, "The Science of Muddling Through," *Public Administration Review* 19 (1959); Herbert Simon, *Administrative Behavior* (New York: Macmillan, 1957).

8. For examples of studies using the same justification to frame elite behavior in terms of rational choice theory, see John Aldrich, *Before the Convention: Strategies and Choices in Presidential Nomination Campaigns* (Chicago: Univ. of Chicago Press, 1980), and Richard Katz, *A Theory of Parties and Electoral Systems* (Baltimore: John Hopkins Univ. Press, 1980).

9. For examples of the use of rational choice theory in political science see Anthony Downs, *An Economic Theory of Democracy* (New York: Harper and Row, 1957); Mancur Olson, *The Logic of Collective Action* (Cambridge, Mass.: Harvard Univ. Press, 1965); William Riker, *The Theory of Political Coalitions* (New Haven, Conn.: Yale Univ. Press, 1962); and William Riker and Peter Ordeshook, *An Introduction to Positive Political Theory* (Englewook Cliffs, N.J.: Prentice-Hall).

10. See Aldrich, *Before the Convention*; Katz, *Theory of Parties*; Barry Weingast, Kenneth Shepsle, and Christopher Johnsen, "The Political Economy of Benefits and Costs: A Neoclassical Approach to the Politics of Distribution," *Journal of Politics* 89 (1981); and Kenneth Shepsle and Barry Weingast, "Political Preferences for the Pork Barrel," *American Journal of Political Science* 79 (1981).

11. Richard F. Fenno, *Congressmen in Committees* (Boston: Little, Brown, 1973), and *Homestyle*; David Mayhew, *Congress: The Electoral Connection* (New Haven, Conn.: Yale Univ. Press, 1974).

12. Fenno, *Congressmen in Committees*, and *Homestyle*. Also see Randall Strahan, "Members' Goals and Coalition-Building Strategies in the U.S. Hous: The Case of Tax Refore," *Journal of Politics* 51 (1989).

13. Kenneth Arrow, *Social Choice and Individual Values*, 2d ed. (New York: Wiley, 1963). Also see Riker and Ordeshook, *Introduction to Positive Theory*.

14. Downs, *Economic Theory of Democracy*.

15. This assumption that political parties exist to pursue the goals of the individuals who comprise it was also made by Katz, *Theory of Parties*.

16. The seminal work in this area is, of course, Max Weber, "Bureaucracy," in *From Max Weber: Essays in Sociology* (New York: Oxford Univ. Press, 1958) ed. H.H. Gerth and C. Wright Mills. Also see James S. Coleman, *Power and the Structure of Society* (New York: Norton, 1973); and Eugene Lewis, *American Politics in a Bureaucratic Age* (Cambridge, Mass.: Winthrop, 1977).

17. See Fenno, *Homestyle*.

18. This is similar to the dilemma facing the parties when reapportioning state legislative or congressional districts. If the party takes territory away from safe districts to increase their chances of gaining a majority, they may endanger individual legislators from those districts.

19. This is known in benefit cost terms as "discounting."

20. The possibility of pure party interests controlling a caucus campaign committee can be found in the practice followed by some senate caucus campaign committees, in which membership is limited to candidates who are not up for reelection.

21. Shepsle and Weingast, "Political Preferences for the Pork Barrel."

22. Ibid.

23. Welch, "Economics of Campaign Funds."

24. See Downs, *Economic Theory of Democracy*; and E.E. Schattschneider, *Party Government* (New York: Holt, Rinehart and Winston, 1942).

25. Several studies have uncovered evidence of strategic behavior on the part of legislative party committees at the national and state level. These include: Herrnson, "Party Strategies and Resource Distribution"; Gary Jacobson and Samuel Kernell, *Strategy and Choice in Congressional Elections* (New Haven, Conn.: Yale Univ. Press, 1983); Rom and Aoki, "How Big the Pig"; and Stonecash, "Working at the Margins."

26. Shepsle and Weingast, "Political Preferences for the Pork Barrel"; and Weingast et al., "Political Economy of Costs and Benefits."

27. Jacobson and Kernell, *Strategy and Choice*, and Herrnson, "Party Strategies and Resource Distribution," provide some evidence of this in their research on the national parties. Stonecash, "Working at the Margins," found a pattern in the distribution of funds by the New York state legislative campaign committees suggesting that party trends affected the allocation of resources. John Chubb, "Institutions, the Economy, and the Dynamics of State Legislative Elections," *American Political Science Review* 82 (1988), found that national forces seem to have an impact on the outcome of state legislative races. Whether these findings are due solely to voting behavior or the behavior of elites, e.g., legislative party decision-makers, remains to be seen.

28. The procedures for obtaining the data are, however, very different. Some states willing shipped summary reports via the mail without any charge, others charge around $10 a volume. For some states it was necessary to obtain photocopies of the expenditure reports of the campaign committees. And some states required that records be obtained in person at the state capitol. The worst case was Illinois, perhaps reflecting its individualistic political culture, where one must complete a form, in triplicate, for each candidate's or organization's committee record reviewed. One of these forms is sent to the candidate or organization. A week following my visit to Illinois I received a letter from the chair of one of the campaign committees noting that they were aware of my investigation of their records.

29. The New York data was provided by Jeffrey Stonecash.

30. See Sorauf, *Money in American Elections*, for a detailed discussion of these problems.

31. Maine was originally to be included in the analysis of the campaign finance data, but the campaign finance records maintained by that state proved insufficiently detailed.

32. Illinois Sentate Minority Leader, James "Pate" Philip, refused to discuss the practices of the Republican State Senate Campaign Committee with me because I was a Democrat. He said he was afraid he would give away "secrets" during an interview.

3. Finances

1. The amount of money available to California legislative party campaign committees clearly puts them in a class by themselves. In 1986 the top six contributors to all campaigns in the state were caucus campaign committees and leadership PACs.

2. For some states, candidates' total revenues were not available, and thus the calculation of percent of total revenues from the campaign committees was impossible.

4. Legislative Party Campaign Committees: Structure and Practices

1. Herrnson, "Party Strategies and Resource Distribution," found that because the DCCC was composed largely of incumbent congressmen, the efficiency with which DCCC funds were allocated was reduced.

2. It is important to remember that all discussion of California legislative party campaign committees refers to past practices. Proposition 73, passed by voters in 1988, has effectively eliminated the committees in California for now.

3. The field workers used to be provided by the state party organization in the 1970s.

4. See Herrnson, *Party Campaigning in the 1980s.*

5. Quoted from testimony given before the New York Commission on Government Integrity on Mar. 17, 1989, reprinted in "A Public Hearing on Campaign Finance Practices," 54.

6. See Herrnson, *Party Campaigning in the 1980s.*

7. See Jewell and Olson, *Political Parties and Elections,* 221-22.

8. Sorauf and Beck, *Party Politics in America.*

9. Supplemental material was provided by the campaign finance records of the caucus campaign committees.

10. A Republican source in the Tennessee House indicated that the practice of legislators transferring funds does not occur in house races; however, a Republican source in the senate stated that such a practice does occur in senate races.

11. See California Commission on Campaign Financing, *The New Gold Rush: Financing California Legislative Campaigns,* (Los Angeles: Center for Responsive Government, 1985).

5. The Allocation of Resources: Competitiveness and Incumbency

1. Respondents indicated that the campaign committees used a variety of indicators to determine the competitiveness of the election, ranging from

sophisticated polling to subjective perceptions regarding the strength of candidates, including demographics research and previous district election results. Most state that the previous margin was one of those indicators. Some committees, such as the Minnesota DFL committees, actually have computer generated "DFL Indexes" for each district based upon how DFL candidates have performed in those districts.

2. The scale was folded in this way so that as competitiveness of a particular race increased so did the measure. Using straight vote percentages obviously is not appropriate because a candidate who won with 51 percent of the vote was in just as close a race as the candidate who lost with 49 percent of the vote. For incumbents, the measure indicates what their margin of victory was in the past election, and for nonincumbents the measure indicates how close their party came to winning or losing the past election.

3. Regressing the vote on the previous vote for each district resulted in R-squares ranging from a high of .78 to a low of .37, with an average R-square of .62. The average margin used in the 1982 analysis performed much better, with an average R-square of .83.

4. This information was obtained in the discussions with legislative leaders and caucus staff members.

5. The correlations between the previous margin and the final outcome of the race, noted in note 3, indicate that the previous margin is a relatively good indicator of the competitiveness of an election.

6. Because all of the regressions use the entire population, significance levels are not very relevant. Significance levels are based upon probability theory involving the relationship between estimated parameters and actual population parameters. The standard errors are included in the tables for those who believe significance tests are still relevant under these conditions. Most of the coefficients are significant. For those that are not, the failure of the coefficient to be twice the size of the standard error is most likely due to the imperfect nature of the measure of competitiveness.

7. Whether the nonlinear model was a better fit for the committee's resource allocation pattern was determined by the size of the coefficient for the square of the competitiveness measure relative to its standard error and by the increase, if any, in the R-square, which indicates the variance explained by the regression model.

8. For an equation in which $y = b_0 + b_1x_1 + b_2x_1^2$ the slope at $x_1 = b_1 + 2b_2x_1$ see William Berry and Stanley Feldman, *Multiple Regression in Practice* (Beverly Hills, Calif.: Sage Publications, 1985), 59-60.

9. This was computed by plugging the coefficients into the equation COMPETITION = $b_1 + 2b_2$ (COMPETITION) and solving it for different values of COMPETITION.

10. In interpreting the results of the analysis of the leadership campaign committees, caution must to exercised to avoid the ecological fallacy of inferring individual behavior from aggregate statistics. The results must be interpreted in terms of the aggregate distributional strategies of legislative leadership PACs in each state.

11. This information was obtained from Rom and Aoki, "How Big the Pig," and from interviews with Wisconsin legislators and staff reported in chapter 4.

12. See note 7 above for an explanation of what constituted a better fit and notes 8 and 9 above for how to interpret the coefficients.

13. See Cotter et al., *Party Organization in American Politics*.

14. A ratio could not be calculated in situations in which one group of candidates did not receive any assistance from a caucus committee because it involved a division by zero. In some cases there were no candidates in a group, thus making a comparison of means inapplicable.

6. Caucus Committees Versus Leadeship PACs

1. The variables are coded "1" if the candidate is from that state and "0" if not. One state is left out because including it would lead to biased estimators. These coefficients are omitted from the tables because they are used merely as controls and lack relevance to the research question.

2. See Eric Hanushek and John E. Jackson, *Statistical Methods for Social Scientists* (New York: Academic Press, 1977), 101-106.

3. Comparison of the nonlinear model coefficients is more complicated because it depends on the relative values of both equations. For the equations with the squared term, the relationship between competitiveness and the proportion of committee funds received depends on the value of the independent variable: $x_1 = b_1 + 2b_2x_1$. Comparing committees that fit different regression models is even more complicated. When the linear model is used for all committees very little difference is evident between any two committees in terms of focusing on competitive races. The nonlinear models are used in Table 6-1 because they represent a better test of the difference between the committees in funding nonincumbents; i.e., it minimizes bias in the coefficients.

4. For the equations with the squared term, the relationship between competitiveness and the proportion of committee funds received is dependent on the value of the independent variable: $x_1 = b_1 + 2b_2x_1$. For the Democrats in 1982, the coefficient for the squared terms (.001 for the caucus committees and .004 for the leadership PACs) in relationship to the coefficient for the competitiveness measure indicates the leadership committees are better at concentrating their resources on close races. When x_1 is 45, the Democratic caucus committees in 1982 were likely to give .041 percent of their funds for each increase a tenth of a percent in the competitiveness of the race; the leadership PACs were likely to give .155 percent.

7. Strategic Variations in Caucus Committee Tactics

1. For evidence of the incumbency advantage at the state level see Jewell and Breaux, "Effect of Incumbency."

2. Evidence of this can be found in the research on the national parties. See chapter 2, note 27.

3. This statement is usually attributed to former U.S. Speaker Tip O'Neall.

4. As in the previous chapter the squared term was included only in cases where it was found to significantly add to the regression model.

5. The rest of the coefficients, the standard errors, the constant, and the R^2 can all be found in the tables in chapter 6.

6. The states that support the contention that minority parties will place a greater emphasis on nonincumbents (states that have a greater coefficient for nonincumbents) are: Wisconsin in 1982; Oregon in 1982, 1984, and 1986; Indiana in 1982 and 1986; New York in 1984 and 1986; Washington in 1984 and 1986; Illinois in 1986.

7. Because the data for the Illinois House Republicans is missing in 1984, nothing can be concluded about their tendency to shift emphasis from nonincumbents to incumbents or vice versa over time.

8. Though the race for governor in 1982 turned out to be close, the important consideration was the expectations regarding partisan performance prior to the election. This, it is argued, is what shapes party decision-making with regard to incumbent and nonincumbent candidates. The expectation prior to the 1982 election was that Thompson would win easily in the race against former U.S. Senator Adlai Stevenson—some polls gave Thompson a margin of 10 percentage points. What pollsters did not consider was the effect of the massive voter registration drive among blacks in the city of Chicago, gearing up for the 1983 mayoral election. The result was an extremely close race with Thompson winning by about 5,000 votes. See Paul Kleppner, *Chicago Divided: The Making of a Black Mayor* (DeKalb, Ill.: Northern Illinois Univ. Press, 1985).

9. The Illinois Senate Republicans refused to discuss the practices of the Republican State Senate Campaign Committee with me.

10. Jacobson and Kernell, *Strategy and Choice.*

11. State party trends were determined by the votes for governor or senator in that year, using the National Journal's *Almanac of American Politics, 1988*. If a gubernatorial or senate candidate received 60 percent of the vote or greater, then that candidate's party was determined to have had a good year. If candidates from both parties won with 60 percent of the vote or greater or if no candidate won with greater than 60 percent, neither party was determined to have a positive trend.

12. Dummy variables for the states are included in the analysis to control for any state variation that might result in biased coefficients from the pooled data set. Substantively it could be argued that these coefficients represent the average proportion of caucus campaign committee funds received by incumbents in noncompetitive races; however, the value of the coefficients also depends on the number of districts in the state, the number of competitive races, etc. Because they represent these idiosyncratic state factors they should not be interpreted as a comparable measure of caucus committee efficiency in terms of funding nonincumbents in close races. Hence, these coefficients will be of little interest and act merely as control variables.

13. For example, when the value of the dummy variable for party status is equal to 0—i.e., the party holds a majority of seats—the value of the coefficient for the nonincumbent variable is the proportion nonincumbents of majority parties receive from the caucus committee. When the dummy variable is equal to 1, the proportion of caucus committee funds a candidate can

expect is equal to the value of the nonincumbent coefficient plus the coefficient of the interaction term. For a further discussion of the use of interaction effects in OLS regression see William Berry and Stanley Feldman, *Multiple Regression in Practice*.

14. Interpretation of the interaction terms requires that the coefficient of the interaction term be added to the coefficient for the base variable. For example, the emphasis placed on nonincumbents for minority parties is equal to the coefficient of the interaction term plus the coefficient for nonincumbents. The emphasis placed on nonincumbents for majority parties is merely the coefficient for the nonincumbent variable. The value of the interaction variable (nonincumbency * party status) for all majority parties is equal to 0 (because party status equals 0 if the party held a majority of seats before the election).

8. Conclusion

1. Herrnson, "Do Parties Make a Difference?" and *Party Campaigning in the 1980s*.

2. See Burnham, *Current Crisis in American Politics*; David E. Price, *Bringing Back the Parties* (Washington, D.C.: Congressional Quarterly Press, 1984); and Crotty, *American Parties in Decline*.

3. See Cornelius Cotter and John Bibby, "Institutional Development and the Thesis of Party Decline," *Political Science Quarterly* 95 (1980): 1-27; Cotter et al., *Party Organizations in American Politics*; Schlesinger, "New American Political Party"; and Herrnson, *Party Campaigning in the 1980s*.

4. Except, of course, the research by Cotter and Bibby, and Cotter et al.

Bibliography

Alexander, Herbert E. 1988. "Initiatives in California Political Finance." *Impact* (July/Aug): 1, 3-4. Arterton, F. Christopher. 1982. "Political Money and Party Strength." In *The Future of American Political Parties: The Challenge of Governance,* ed. Joel L. Fleishman. Englewood Cliffs, N.J.: Prentice Hall.

Bibby, John. 1979. "Political Parties and Federalism: The Republican National Committee Involvement in Gubernatorial and Legislative Elections." *Publius* 9: 229-36.

Bibby, John. 1983. "Patterns in Midterm Gubernatorial and State Legislative Elections." *Public Opinion* (Feb./Mar.): 41-46.

Biersack, Robert, and Clyde Wilcox. 1989. "The Role of Campaign Finance in the Electoral Process." Paper presented at the 1989 Annual Meeting of the Midwest Political Science Association.

Boyd, William. 1982. "Campaign Finance and Electoral Outcomes in Wisconsin and Georgia House Races." Paper delivered at the Annual Meeting of the Midwest Political Science Association.

Breaux, David, and Anthony Gierzynski. 1990. "Money in State Legislative Elections." Paper presented at the Lexington Conference on State Legislative Elections.

Burnham, Walter Dean. 1982. *The Current Crisis in American Politics.* New York: Oxford Univ. Press.

Caldeira, Gregory A., and Samuel C. Patterson. 1982. "Bringing Home the Votes: Electoral Outcomes in State Legislative Races." *Political Behavior* 4: 33-67.

California Commission on Campaign Financing. 1985. *The New Gold Rush: Financing California Legislative Campaigns.* Los Angeles: Center for Responsive Government.

Chubb, John E. 1988. "Institutions, the Economy, and the Dynamics of State Elections." *American Political Science Review* 82: 133-54.

Clucas, Richard. 1989. "Campaign Support as a Leadership Resource: A Case Study of Two California Assembly Speakers." Paper presented at the Annual Meeting of the American Political Science Association.

Collie, Melissa P. 1988. "The Legislature and Distributive Policy Making in Formal Perspective." *Legislative Studies Quarterly* 13: 427-58.

Cotter, Cornelius P., and John F. Bibby. 1980. "Institutional Development and the Thesis of Party Decline." *Political Science Quarterly* 95: 1-27.

Cotter, Cornelius P., James L. Gibson, John F. Bibby, and Robert J. Huckshorn. 1984. *Party Organizations in American Politics.* New York: Praeger.

Crotty, William J. 1984. *American Parties in Decline.* Boston: Little, Brown.

Downs, Anthony. 1957. *An Economic Theory of Democracy*. New York: Harper and Row.

Drew, Elizabeth. 1983. *Politics and Money: The New Road to Corruption*. New York: Macmillan.

Eisenstein, James. 1984. "Patterns of Campaign Finance in Pennsylvania's 1982 Legislative Elections." Paper delivered at the Annual Meeting of the Pennsylvania Political Science Association.

Fenno, Richard F. 1973. *Congressmen in Committees*. Boston: Little, Brown.

Fenno, Richard F. 1978. *Home Style: House Members in Their Districts*. Boston: Little, Brown.

Gierzynski, Anthony, and David Breaux. "Money and Votes in State Legislative Elections." *Legislative Quarterly* 16

Gierzynski, Anthony, and Malcolm Jewell. n.d. "Legislative Caucus and Leadership Campaign Committees." In *State Legislative Career Patterns*, ed. Gary Moncrief and Joel Thompson. Forthcoming from Univ. of Michigan Press.

Gierzynski, Anthony, and Malcolm Jewell. 1989. "Legislative Party Campaign Finance Activity: A Comparative State Analysis." Paper Presented at the Annual Meeting of the Midwest Political Science Association.

Gierzynski, Anthony, and Malcolm Jewell. 1989. "Legislative Party and Leadership Campaign Committees: An Analysis of Resource Allocation. Paper presented at the Annual Meeting of the American Political Science Association.

Giles, Micheal W., and Anita Pritchard. 1985. "Campaign Expenditures and Legislative Elections in Florida." *Legislative Studies Quarterly* 10: 71-88.

Green, Donald Philip, and Jonathan S. Krasno. 1988. "Salvation for the Spendthrift Incumbent: Reestimating the Effects of Campaign Spending in House Elections." *American Journal of Political Science* 32: 884-907.

Herrnson, Paul S. n.d. "Party Strategies and Resource Distribution in the 1984 Congressional Elections." Department of Political Science, University of Massachusetts at Amherst. Manuscript.

Herrnson, Paul S. 1986. "Do Parties Make a Difference? The Role of Party Organizations in Congressional Elections." *Journal of Politics* 48: 589-615.

Herrnson, Paul S. 1988. *Party Campaigning in the 1980s*. Cambridge, Mass.: Harvard Univ. Press.

Huckshorn, Robert J., and John F. Bibby. 1982. "State Parties in an Era of Political Change." In *The Future of American Political Parties: The Challenge of Governance*, ed. Joel L. Fleishman. Englewood Cliffs, N.J.: Prentice Hall.

Jacobson, Gary C. 1980. *Money in Congressional Elections*. New Haven, Conn.: Yale Univ. Press.

Jacobson, Gary C. 1985. "Money and Votes Reconsidered: Congressional Elections 1972-1982." *Public Choice* 47: 7-92.

Jacobson, Gary C. 1985. "Party Organization and Distribution of Campaign Resources: Republicans and Democrats in 1982." *Political Science Quarterly* 4: 603-25.

Jacobson, Gary C. 1985. "Parties and PACs in Congressional Elections." In *Congress Reconsidered*, ed. Lawrence Dodd and Bruce Oppenheimer. Washington, D.C.: Congressional Quarterly Press.

Jacobson, Gary C., and Samuel Kernell. 1983. *Strategy and Choice in Congressional Elections.* 2d ed. New Haven, Conn.: Yale Univ. Press.

Jewell, Malcolm. 1986. "A Survey of Campaign Fund Raising by Legislative Parties." *Comparative State Politics Newsletter,* 9-13.

Jewell, Malcolm. 1987. "The Prospects for Nationalizing State Legislative Elections." *Electoral Politics,* 12-15.

Jewell, Malcolm, and David Breaux. 1989. "The Effect of Incumbency On State Legislative Elections." *Legislative Studies Quarterly* 13, no. 4: 495-510.

Jewell, Malcolm, and David Olson. 1988. *American State Political Parties and Elections.* Homewood, Ill.: Dorsey Press.

Johnson, Richard R. 1987. "Partisan Legislative Campaign Committees: New Power, New Problems." *Illinois Issues* (July): 16-18.

Jones, Ruth. 1984. "Financing State Elections." In *Money and Politics in the United States,* ed. Michael Malbin. Chatham, N.J.: Chatham House.

Jones, Ruth, and Thomas J. Borris. 1985. "Strategic Contributing in Legislative Campaigns: The Case of Minnesota." *Legislative Studies Quarterly* 10: 89-105.

Kayden, Xandra. 1980. "The Nationalization of the Party System." In *Parties, Interest Groups, and Campaign Finance Laws,* ed. Michael J. Malbin. Washington, D.C.: American Enterprise Institute.

Leyden, Kevin, and Stephen Borrelli. 1987. "Party Contributions and Party Unity: Can Loyalty Be Bought?" Paper delivered at the Annual Meeting of the Southern Political Science Association.

March, James, and Johan Olson. 1984. "The New Institutionalism: Organizational Factors in Political Life." *American Political Science Review* 78: 734-49.

Mayhew, David R. 1974. *Congress: The Electoral Connection.* New Haven, Conn.: Yale Univ. Press.

New York Commission on Government Integrity. Mar. 17, 1989. "A Public Hearing on Campaign Finance Practices." Albany, NY.

Patterson, Samuel C., and Malcolm E. Jewell. 1984. "Elections in the American States." Paper delivered at the Research Planning Conference on Comparative State Politics, Stanford University.

Price, David E. 1984. *Bringing Back the Parties.* Washington, D.C.: Congressional Quarterly Press.

Ranney, Austin. 1976. "Parties in State Politics." In *Politics in the American States: A Comparative Analysis,* ed. Herbert Jacobs and Kenneth Vines. 3d ed. Boston: Little, Brown.

Rom, Mark, and Andrew Aoki. 1987. "How Big the Pig: Wisconsin Campaign Contributions, Legislative Vote Scores, and the Party in Government." Paper delivered at the Annual Meeting of the Northeast Political Science Association.

Rose, Gary L. 1987. "Party Organization Activity in the 1986 Connecticut State Legislative Election." Paper delivered at the Annual Meeting of the Northeast Political Science Association.

Rosenthal, Alan. 1987. "The Legislative Institution: Transformation and/or Decline." Paper delivered at the State of the State Symposium.

Sartori, Giovanni. 1976. *Parties and Party Systems: A Framework for Analysis,* vol. 1. Cambridge, Mass.: Cambridge Univ. Press.

Schattschneider, E. E. 1942. *Party Government.* Holt, Rinehart and Winston.

Schlesinger, Joseph A. 1984. "On the Theory of Party Organization." *Journal of Politics* 46: 369-400.

Schlesinger, Joseph A. 1985. "The New American Political Party." *American Political Science Review* 79: 1152-69.

Shepsle, Kenneth, and Barry R. Weingast. 1981. "Institutionalizing Majority Rule: A Social Choice Theory with Policy Implications." *American Economic Review* 72: 367-71.

Shepsle, Kenneth, and Barry Weingast. 1981. "Political Preferences for the Pork Barrel." *American Journal of Political Science* 25: 96-111.

Sorauf, Frank J. 1963. *Party and Representation*. New York: Atherton.

Sorauf, Frank J. 1988. *Money in American Elections*. Glenview, Ill.: Scott, Foresman.

Stonecash, Jeffrey. 1989. "Working at the Margins: Campaign Finance and Party Strategy in New York Assembly Elections." *Legislative Studies Quarterly* 13, no. 4.

Stonecash, Jeffrey M., and Thomas D'Agostino. 1987. "Working at the Margins: Campaign Finance and Party Strategy in New York Legislative Elections." Paper delivered at the Annual Meeting of the Southern Political Science Association.

Weingast, Barry R., Kenneth A. Shepsle, and Christopher Johnsen. 1981. "The Political Economy of Benefits and Costs: A Neoclassical Approach to the Politics of Distribution." *Journal of Political Economy* 89: 642-64.

Welch, William P. 1974. "The Economics of Campaign Funds." *Public Choice* 20: 83-97.

Welch, William P. 1976. "The Effectiveness of Expenditures in State Legislative Races." *American Politics Quarterly* 4: 333-56.

Welch, William P. 1977. "The Allocation of Political Monies: Parties, Ideological Groups, and Economic Interest Groups." Working Paper no. 72, Department of Economics, University of Pittsburgh.

Wilcox, Clyde. 1988. "Share the Wealth: Contributions by Congressional Incumbents To the Campaigns of Other Candidates." Paper presented at the Annual Meeting of the American Political Science Association.

Index

www.ingramcontent.com/pod-product-compliance
Lightning Source LLC
Chambersburg PA
CBHW031515270326
41930CB00006B/404